MW00397564

Bluewater Sailing on a Budget

Bluewater Sailing on a Budget

How to Find and Buy a Cruising Sailboat
for Under $50,000—Featuring 20 Seaworthy Boats

Jim Elfers

INTERNATIONAL MARINE / McGRAW-HILL EDUCATION

Camden, Maine • New York • Chicago • San Francisco • Lisbon • London • Madrid
Mexico City • Milan • New Delhi • San Juan • Seoul • Singapore • Sydney • Toronto

For Justin, Bryan, Catherine, Caroline, Cullen, and Patrick.
May you always pursue your dreams whether on land or sea.

Copyright © 2015 by International Marine/ McGraw-Hill Education, LLC. All rights reserved. Printed in the United States of America. Except as permitted under the United States Copyright Act of 1976, no part of this publication may be reproduced or distributed in any form or by any means, or stored in a database or retrieval system, without the prior written permission of the publisher. The name "International Marine" and all associated logos are trademarks of McGraw-Hill Education. The publisher takes no responsibility for the use of any of the materials or methods described in this book, nor for the products thereof.

 2 3 4 5 6 7 8 9 10 QFR/QFR 1 9 8 7 6 5
ISBN 9780071808033
MHID 0-07-180803-5
E ISBN 0-07-180804-3

Library of Congress Cataloging-in-Publication Data is available from the Library of Congress.

McGraw-Hill Education books are available at special quantity discounts to use as premiums and sales promotions or for use in corporate training programs. To contact a representative, please e-mail us at bulksales@ mcgraw-hill.com.

Questions regarding the content of this book should be addressed to www.internationalmarine.com

Questions regarding the ordering of this book should be addressed to
McGraw-Hill Education
Customer Service Department
P.O. Box 547
Blacklick, OH 43004
Retail customers: 1-800-262-4729
Bookstores: 1-800-722-4726

Contents

Foreword

*Life is what happens to
you while you're busy
making other plans.*

—JOHN LENNON

When I was 12 years old, my father, a diplomat, was dispatched to the United States embassy in Madagascar. As was the custom then and now, the diplomat's entire family was packed up and sent along for the two-year stint abroad.

Just before we left, and for reasons that to this day are not clear to me, I used all my disposable income at the time to prepay a one-year subscription to *Sail* magazine. Somehow I even entered the APO address for foreign delivery correctly, and my issue would reach me only three months late at our house in Tananarive. Receiving the August issue in November did not trouble me in the least because I never tired of reading about what seemed to me the ultimate lifestyle—sailing around the world on one's own sailboat.

I was equally untroubled by the fact that I did not know how to sail, had never been sailing, and had no immediate prospects to be able to afford a world cruiser. In those days writers like Herb Payson and the Pardeys stoked a fire in me that would burn to this day, as it has for many others.

By the skin of my teeth, I made it through sixteen years of education, and, after a short period crewing on a megayacht in the Med, built my own cruising trimaran and headed for Mexico. I was 24 years old and had $400 to my name. My first cruise lasted only five months and 2,000 miles, but when I returned to San Diego with $40 and a smile on my face, I knew cruising was something I wanted to try again. Maybe not in a boat with an 8 horsepower diesel, and maybe with a little more money, but I definitely wanted to revisit the cruising lifestyle.

Twenty-five years and 30,000 nautical miles later, I suppose I have accumulated a few tidbits of knowledge worth sharing. I don't have as many sea miles as some, but I have spent my entire career either skippering, delivering, fixing, or surveying boats. But given that there are so many books in print, some incredibly comprehensive and detailed, what niche is it that I am trying to fill here?

This book does not go into detail about the nuances of why a skeg-supported rudder may be more desirable than a spade, or a cutter rig better than a sloop. Instead I have elected to concentrate on specific advice about the search process and the buying process, and then a list of twenty boats (and one honorable mention) that can cruise and are priced accessibly. There are a few similar books out there, but they seem to lean heavily toward full-keel designs and frankly show an East Coast bias. How can one write a book about great production cruising boats and not include a single Cal, or Islander, or Ericson? It seemed to me that the literature was still lacking something.

For many of the last twenty-five years, I have been based at a cruising crossroads, including the last seven years as manager of a major marina in the tropics. The Cape of Baja California in Mexico—known to tourists as Cabo San Lucas—is a unique spot. It is the first place where one can truly hang a left after voyaging down from Alaska or California. It is also the first major downwind port after leaving San Diego, so nearly all cruisers make a stopover in the region.

On one occasion I saw three circumnavigating boats there at the same time, all of very different designs and all finishing their voyages. Talking to cruisers about their boats and the cruising life is something I never tire of; after all, someone always has a tip, an insight, or an experience that is useful. And something about cruising attracts some very interesting people—those who have willfully traded stability for change, the known for the unknown, the routine for the new challenge.

This book gives clear-cut advice as to how one can get into cruising without being rich, and draws on my own observations of hundreds of different cruising boats I have seen and their crews I have talked with. I can't pretend to be as familiar with as many East Coast production sailboats, but at least a few are represented here, chosen more from reputation than personal experience.

The boat purchase budget has a ceiling of $50,000 because anyone who really wants to go badly enough can come up with this amount—if not immediately, then certainly within a few years. Other selection parameters are informed by my own biases—which, while considerable, are not, I like to think, unreasonable.

On the surface, it would seem that you need the following four ingredients to go cruising—the desire, the boat, some sailing experience, and a year's worth of cruising funds. The truth is that only the first two items are indispensable; the last two are nice but their lack will not necessarily stop a determined individual. For those who have that first indispensable ingredient—the desire—I hope this book helps you fulfill the dream.

Stalking the Dream

*The only difference
between a rut and a grave
are the dimensions.*

—Ann Landers

My first big cruise was as a deckhand on a large yacht in the Mediterranean. Fresh out of college, I had received an offer to crew for a family out of California circumnavigating on their 96-foot cutter. Sailing from Corsica down to Sardinia for the 12-meter World Championships, I learned perhaps the most important lesson about cruising the world on a sailboat.

Porto Cervo, at the northern tip of the island of Sardinia, was fast becoming a jet-set capital for yachting. It was being developed by a consortium led by the Agha Khan, and when we pulled in on our big Sparkman and Stephens design we looked pretty small anchored near his mammoth motoryacht. His yacht had a helicopter and a crew of twelve. One of its three tenders was a 50-foot Cigarette speedboat. But the Agha Khan took an interest in our sailboat and invited the owners over for the obligatory 5 o'clock cocktail hour.

Some of the other crew members joined me in going ashore and walking the marina perimeter, which was chockablock full of swanky shops and restaurants. The Costa Esmeralda Yacht Club was crawling with yachties, sheiks, and deck apes wearing shirts intentionally one size too small. Eventually I got bored talking about the nuances of carbon fiber spinnaker poles and managed to sneak outside.

Off in the distance, in the free anchorage north of the marina area, I could see one particularly modest-looking cruiser. It was a trimaran flying a British flag. The little homebuilt plywood dinghy tied to the stern told me that the skipper was aboard. So I asked my compatriots still at the yacht club if I could borrow our yacht's big inflatable for a while, and I motored over. Something about seeing that little boat anchored amidst all the megayachts just fascinated me, and I had to meet the owner.

"Ahoy the trimaran!" I shouted as I got in close enough. "Anyone aboard?"

I heard some shuffling and muttering from below, and after a few seconds a bearded face emerged from the companionway.

"Who wants to know?" he demanded.

"Oh, hey, I'm really sorry to bother you, but I'm thinking about building a multihull and was really fascinated to see your boat here. I mean, how far have you come in this boat?"

"Came from England and am headed for the Red Sea. Come aboard and poke around if you want to."

The boat was maybe 35 feet long, and the owner, Nigel, turned out to be quite a character. His galley was a two-burner stove and was stocked with nothing but a sack of flour, a sack of rice, and a sack of couscous. Nigel had found the boat partially completed and rotting away in a farmer's field. He had traded a car for it, finished it up, and set sail with a few hundred British pounds stashed away on board.

"Been out cruising about a year now," he told me. "The marinas in the Med can be pricey, but if you know what you're doing, there are places to anchor out. Half the time the richer sailors invite me over for lunch or dinner, so sometimes things are pretty nice!"

I had to admit, sitting there in a cramped but cozy cabin, that Nigel seemed every bit as content as some of the megayacht owners I encountered every day.

He was maybe even more relaxed than they were—probably because Nigel did not have to stress about crew salaries, slip fees, and tight schedules.

When I stepped into the dinghy to return to the big boat a half hour later, I was fortunate to have learned a critical lesson early in my cruising career—the happiness index for a cruiser is not directly proportional to the length of his or her boat, or the balance in the bank account.

It is an important lesson. Having spent most of my career in Cabo San Lucas, Mexico—as mentioned previously, this is the first major downwind cruising stop leaving the West Coast of the United States—I can attest to the fact that it is not always the fanciest boat with the latest gear that is having the best time cruising.

Fortunately for prospective cruisers, there have been two parallel phenomena occurring in the U.S. recreational boating market over the past ten years. First, there are more and more older boats coming onto the used boat market that are still very serviceable. The gelcoat may be faded, and six inches of growth may be hanging off the bottom, but except in the smallest sizes these fiberglass boats are not being carried off to wrecking yards like an old Buick of the same vintage. The fact is that fiberglass deteriorates only very slowly over time, and most sailboats over 30 feet have reliable diesels that can last decades.

In other words, much to the delight of marina managers, old boats really don't have a place to go to die. Typically these older boats get sold even more cheaply as each owner tires of paying slip fees and maintenance costs, or because the fire to go cruising that burned brightly for a while is now reduced to ashes. An owner can try to reduce his monthly boat nut by putting the boat in dry storage, or a cheaper marina where his boat can sit in mud half the time, but eventually the boat will be resold.

The second part of the phenomena is that more and more people want to try cruising. Or, perhaps more accurately, they want to escape from a world of mortgages, car payments, 401K worries, and hours a day staring at the rear bumper of the car in front of them. What Thoreau said over a century ago still rings true—the great mass of men do lead lives of quiet desperation.

In the Foreword I stipulated that to go cruising you need, ideally, a boat, the desire, some sailing experience, and cruising funds. Keeping in mind my opinion that only the first two on the list are indispensable, here are some of the things I have seen with my own eyes over the years:

A beautiful brand-new 60-foot cutter, owned by a very young dot.com millionaire who had never cruised before but was on his way to the South Pacific with a girlfriend who looked like she fell out of the pages of *Vogue* magazine.

A wife in her thirties with a young son who came up to my marina office one day to say that she was terrified that she and her husband were about to leave for the Marquesas in their 32-footer. She told me that it was his dream, not hers, and she seemed to be looking for a way out. The next day the boat did leave, and apparently did make it, but they were surviving at least partially on handouts from fellow cruisers.

A singlehander who stayed a few days in the marina aboard her Dana 24, *Might Mary*. The fearless skipper (Mary) was a 64-year-old grandmother, and she ended up cruising extensively.

A couple whom I had never met who had been trying to head north against the prevailing winds. They told me they had reservations for a flight to Los Angeles in 24 hours and then handed me the keys to their beautiful yacht. They had no more interest in cruising and heard that I was a delivery skipper. I ended up singlehanding the 900 miles back.

Cruising is many different things. Cruising is having the dawn watch and seeing the first glimmers of orange light up the cloud bank on the eastern horizon. Cruising is spending two hours on your knees bent over a hot engine while you try to troubleshoot a fuel problem as you enter a new port. Cruising is knowing the instant you hear their breathing that there are dolphins playing on your bow wave even before you see them. Cruising is spending all day in taxis with no air-conditioning going to a series of hardware stores in a country that speaks X in order to find part Y. If you're lucky you may find part Y. If not you will have to make do with part Z instead, or go the next two months without refrigeration, or an autopilot, or whatever else you may have installed on board.

The Cruising Life

Here are some of the key things I hope to convey about cruising.

Some people love it. Others, not so much. With apologies to Jeff Foxworthy, if you grew up surfing in California and could live the rest of your life on just fish tacos and beer, you might be a cruiser. If you are a retired auto mechanic who has sailed his Catalina 42 on San Francisco Bay twenty weekends per year, you might just be a cruiser. If you bought a shiny new 50-footer having never sailed before, but you drank the Cruising Kool-Aid and have convinced yourself that cruising was the retirement you wanted—well, it may end up badly. But don't jump to conclusions. If you are a stressed-out female tax attorney recently divorced and not interested in another relationship for a while, you just might be a cruiser too!

Over the years I have met several hundred cruisers of all types, sometimes when I was out myself but more often as they passed through the port where I was based at the time. The successful long-term cruisers did seem to display a few common traits, but you might be surprised to know that great sailing ability was not always on that list. More common characteristics were a deep and abiding love of the ocean, a "glass-half-full" outlook on everything, and sheer stubbornness or force of will. Sailing ability was rarely as important as fix-it ability, which is not to say that I don't think cruisers really need to be good sailors—just that there are quite a few who do well even if they don't know how to play a lift off the shoreline or rig and fly a spinnaker.

Once I met a Canadian who had just finished a circumnavigation on his Maple Leaf 48. When I noticed he didn't have a pole stowed anywhere, I asked him what he did if he had to run dead downwind.

"I hate poles," he told me. "So I don't go dead downwind. If my destination is dead downwind, I prefer to jibe my way to the port. I find that it doesn't much affect my passage times."

In other words, there are numerous ways to get it done. I have met bluewater cruisers who use their engines even when they could sail at 4 knots, while others had enough fuel for only a few hours of motoring. Some planned and outfitted for a coastal cruise of only a few months but ended up circumnavigating. As far as not getting it done, I have also met many owners who have outfitted their boat with everything imaginable and ended up selling their boat at a significant loss since cruising did not work out for them. In fact, there are far more of this type—those who ultimately will never go—than those who do go.

Timing is everything. The majority of cruisers are retired couples in their fifties or sixties. Some of those I have talked to said that they wish they could have gone when they were younger, but they did not have the money, or careers and families got in the way. Some were very happy they waited since they wanted their kids to have a traditional, stable education, and they were still healthy. A few were very young couples who wanted to get their cruising dream fulfilled before embarking on careers or raising kids. But still others said they went cruising specifically because they had kids!

So you need to choose a moment—or more like a year—that makes sense for your specific scenario. And note that, with recent economic events, many cruisers are changing their attitudes about casually surrendering their jobs to go bluewater cruising. There was a time when you could drop out of the workforce, cruise for a year or two, and then easily reenter the workforce. Those days may be gone forever unless you are a nurse or a software wizard. If you have the boat, the desire, and almost enough money to retire—but could also go right away if you were willing to work again—it may be best to stick it out a few more years. That way you won't even have to worry about finding work again. Yes there is a slight chance that your health may fail or pirates may encroach even farther into your planned cruising grounds, but if it is only a few years, my advice would be to use a picture of Bora Bora as your screensaver and stick it out in any good-paying job until you are pretty sure your cruising can be "open ended." And what a sense of freedom that day will bring.

Of course, if you hate your boss or your job and are in danger of going postal, head down to Costco and start loading up the boat tomorrow. You may return to a career change flipping burgers, but at least you will have made your dream voyage—and can show your photos to the kid working the deep fryer next to you.

The choice is yours. When and whether you go depends entirely on how deep inside you the fire burns to set sail. If you want to find excuses not to go, you can. If you have the drive to overcome all the obstacles that may be thrown your way, you will. For some people, myself included, the ocean and sailing are addictions as strong as the most potent heroin.

To me a cruising sailboat serves like an enabler, a tool allowing me access to the Water Planet. Like other junkies, I have sometimes hoped that the addiction would fade as the years went by, but it hasn't. I remember once, when I was driving my VW bug across the country to start my freshman year in college, I spent a night at a rest stop in Kansas. Others had RVs with comfy beds and accoutrements not unlike those on a modern yacht, but at age 17 all I could afford was a two-person tent. It was a windy night, and as I crawled out of my little home in the morning a big gust ripped the tent out of my hand and started blowing it across the prairie.

Luckily the tent eventually fetched up on a barbed wire fence, but as I ran up to it and looked around to check if anyone had noticed, I saw nothing but flat crop fields everywhere I looked. There wasn't even a tree in sight, just a few bushes back at the rest stop and the interstate cutting through the brown panorama. For the first time I realized that I was about as far from salt water as you could get within the continent—over a thousand miles in any direction.

My hands started to shake. My skin felt clammy. I ran back to my car with the tent in tow, collapsed it in a mad rush, stuffed it under the hood (a VW bug, remember), and continued driving westward. I knew that with every passing mile I was getting closer to the Pacific, an ocean I had only briefly visited but, after this trip, knew I wouldn't leave for very long for the rest of my life.

Thirty-three years later, as I was writing this book, I sold number seven in a long line of cruising sailboats that I had owned. Most were bought cheap, fixed up, and cruised. But a few, in all honesty, had spent way too much time at the dock while I plotted some way to escape from the usual commitments of jobs, family, and "being responsible." This time, after I had the check from the yacht broker in my hand, I told myself I needed to forget about cruising until the boys had finished high school and I had some idea of what might sustain me into retirement. This time the money would be deposited somewhere safe, and I would go boatless for the first time in my adult life. No more slip fees, mechanics bills, yard charges, insurance, or sanding.

One week after I deposited the check, I was on the Internet looking at boats. Just in case. Just checking. After all, I wouldn't want to miss out on a great deal, right?

The Goldilocks Cruiser

Whether you think you can or you think you can't, you're right.

—Henry Ford

So just what is your "Goldilocks cruiser"? Not too big, or too small, or too expensive? If you read some of the other literature, you see that the most aggressive advice will be that your Goldilocks cruiser is whatever you own right now. "Just untie the dock lines and go," they say. Others will tell you that you are foolish to go sailing with anything less than 40 feet in length, equipped with radar, refrigeration, solar panels, and so forth. My advice falls somewhere in between.

If you own a boat now and you are comfortable with it—and especially if it is paid off and not likely to recover anywhere near your investment if you sold it—then by all means you may already have the right boat for your circumstances. You can concentrate on outfitting it with what you need to fulfill your cruising plans, start collecting freedom chips (cash in the bank), and go when you are ready.

If you don't own a boat, or you are sure that the one you have is inadequate, then I would suggest you start by establishing a certain attitude toward cruising in general and boat ownership in particular—bearing in mind that the advice reflects my own experiences and biases.

Will You Own the Boat or Will the Boat Own You?

Allow me to describe a remarkably common scenario. I have seen it play out time and time again, so it bears repeating here.

Wally Wanderlust has dreamed about sailing off to blue skies and warm waters his entire life. For almost thirty years he worked hard to put his kids through school, earn a pension, and live responsibly. A few years before his retirement, he convinced his partner, Holly Hesitant, to sell their house and move onto a beautiful 45-foot sailboat that they purchased in anticipation of cruising.

They settle into the marina life, and even Holly seems to take to the new environment. She feeds the marina ducks every day, teaches her cat how to get in and out of the cabin, and makes friends with the other marina liveaboards.

Meanwhile Wally has become a regular at the local chandlery. He gobbles up the cruising magazines to make sure he has the latest gadgetry, surfs the Internet until 2 a.m. burning up his credit card, and hires local marine contractors to perform installations that are beyond his confidence level. Soon their stock 45-footer sprouts a radar arch with davits, an insulated backstay for the new ham radio, a watermaker, a cockpit dodger, and a bimini. A $3,000 RIB (rigid inflatable) dinghy with outboard is next, then the same amount for a feathering propeller, and by the time they feel that they are ready, almost $80,000 USD has been spent outfitting their $220,000 boat. But no matter, at least they are ready, and a date is set.

Wally and Holly set sail for Mexico on *Gotta Go* with aspirations for a South Pacific cruise. They have only $50,000 cash left in the bank from the $350,000 they started with, but they do have pension income of $24,000 per year that they hope will help keep them going. By the time they clear San Diego for Mexico, they have gotten some of the bugs out of the boat.

But given that they were too busy installing systems rather than proving the boat and themselves in test sails, *Gotta Go* is showing some weaknesses.

The 800-mile shakedown cruise to Cabo San Lucas proves especially trying for Holly, who enjoyed living aboard at the marina but had never done even a coastal ocean passage. By the time they reach Cabo San Lucas, she has been seasick for most of the trip, and cold and scared during most of the night watches. Even her husband, the alpha male, is having misgivings. But he has invested so much financially in the boat and emotionally in his cruising dream that he feels like he has no choice but to push on.

Before I get the female sailors out there too miffed, let me say that this is just the typical scenario I have seen. There are also instances where the female half of a cruising couple has more desire to keep going than the male does. And I have seen some boats where the female is the skipper and the male is less competent as a sailor, but by and large it is the male on board who is the driving force behind a cruise.

This creates even more than just the usual stress on a marriage since the woman is taken away from all that she is comfortable with (family, friends, a meaningful job, shopping malls, and terra firma) and almost overnight plunged into the wet, rolling, unfamiliar world of cruising. Her entire world has been condensed into 40 feet of fiberglass. Just going to the bathroom when the boat is under way is a feat of both agility and marksmanship.

Wally convinces Holly to keep going, but more breakdowns occur, to the point that they start to believe the saying that "cruising is yacht maintenance in exotic ports." They have some good times, too, as the water warms up and they enter the tropics, but when Christmas arrives they feel uncomfortable leaving the boat alone in Central America and don't want to spend the money for expensive tickets to return stateside. Finally they reach Panama, where it is hot and buggy and where they realize they haven't seen their grandkids in almost a year. They also accept that they may not have it in them to make the long passage to the Galapagos and the South Pacific.

Wally and Holly join many other would-be cruisers at the dock of broken dreams. The boat goes on an already glut-

TWO COST SCENARIOS FOR A $250,000 BUDGET

$125,000 Boat Example
50% Boat Purchase/25% Outfitting and Marina Fees/25% Cash Reserves

Starting Capital	$250,000
Cost of Boat	-125,000
Outfitting	- 65,000
Cash Reserves	$60,000
ROI on boat if sold at 30% loss	$133,000
Total return on investment (ROI) prior to considering actual cruising costs	**$193,000**

$62,500 Boat Example
25% Boat Purchase/20% Outfitting and Marina Fees/55% Cash Reserves

Starting Capital	$250,000
Cost of Boat	-62,500
Outfitting	-50,000
Cash Reserves	$137,500
ROI on boat if sold at 40% loss	$67,500
Total ROI prior to considering actual cruising costs	**$205,000**

ted market and in a remote location. Without their care (they have flown back to the States), the humid climate of Central America takes a toll on the equipment and cosmetics. The boat sells, eventually, for a fraction of what they have invested.

To avoid this sort of scenario, one should ask from the beginning—*are we going to own our boat or is our boat going to own us?* To put it another way, unless you have already cruised and know what is involved, I highly suggest you avoid committing more resources than necessary to any contemplated voyage. I would even go so far as to suggest a percentage amount based on total cash assets and any monthly pension benefits. My recommendation would be to spend not more than about a third of your total net worth on a cruising boat. And if you are close to retirement, even less than that unless you have a monthly pension that will easily handle your new lifestyle.

Note that the second scenario (shown at left) considers a 40 percent loss on the investment in the boat once it is resold since it is assumed that the boat will be considerably older than that in Example One. But in the second example, $137,500 is still held in cash, while in the first scenario only $60,000 is cash. If there is a family emergency, a change of plans, or another drastic change in reality, the owners of the boat in the second scenario are in a much better position because they have not overcommitted financially to their cruising aspirations.

Additionally I have seen that cruisers with a little lower percentage of their overall worth invested in the boat are more comfortable anchoring out, less worried about a catastrophic loss such as in a hurricane, and in general are able to see their craft as more of a tool for newfound freedom rather than an obsession that has to be constantly fussed over. Other benefits to a lower boat purchase cost include better insurance rates and, if you have purchased a 40-footer when you could have afforded a bigger boat, lower slip fees.

In 2008 renowned cruisers Lin and Larry Pardey had a three-week stopover in Apia, Samoa, and used the opportunity to informally poll the eighty or so cruisers who were there. What they discovered about the stress levels of the "budget" boats was interesting.

"Every respondent told of spending 25 to 35 percent of the boat's purchase price to make it ready for a voyage across the Pacific. The affordable-boat-fleet owners tended to be closer to 35 percent. Were they as happy with their boats as those who had spent far more money for newer boats? It may just have been our impression, but they seemed to be more content with their choice (i.e., not yet looking toward "the next boat"), more carefree, and less concerned about money. More of the sailors in this group went out to join the local fun races in Neiafu. All definitely had lower expenses and far lower insurance premiums. In fact, three of these couples had chosen not to sell their homes and put the majority of their resources into a boat. Thus, since their boats represented only a limited portion of their assets, they did not feel they had to carry insurance for crossing oceans."

Hopefully by now it is obvious that I would always recommend buying a used boat that leaves something in the kitty for actual cruising. Just like cars, boats lose a lot of value the minute they are delivered to you and go from new to used status. But boats are very much different from cars in almost all other respects as far as resale goes, and in many ways a used boat is actually a better option than a brand-new one. Other than just the obvious devaluation that has occurred over time, the older boat you will want is going to be fiberglass and will have a diesel engine. Neither the fiberglass nor the engine will be seriously affected by a decade of typical recreational use.

A strong case can be made that it takes two to five years just to work out the bugs in a new boat, add desired gear, and in general get comfortable with your acquisition. If you are lucky you will find a boat that has had a lot of expensive cruising gear already installed. It is not uncommon to find great buys on older boats that have sailed maybe only twice a year for ten years but have good radars, biminis, autopilots, extra sails, and so forth. In these cases you may have to increase the initial purchase budget somewhat, but you will be able to decrease your outfitting budget to compensate.

Now back to the premise of this book: Is it really possible to get a cruising boat for under $50,000? Absolutely, especially if you accept the idea that you own the boat and the boat will not be owning you. Of course a truly outfitted cruising boat at a bargain price will go fast, so the next chapter will give some tips on the search process. But first let's finish narrowing down what we will be looking for in our cruiser.

We can start with boat size. Nothing is more fundamental, as this decision will inform everything from slip fees to anchor size to insurance costs. In the 1970s the average cruising boat length was less than 35 feet. In the 1980s and 1990s, the length crept up to almost 40 feet, and today, although I still see boats in the 35- to 40-foot range, I see even more that are over 40 feet. My best guess is that the average length is now just under 45 feet for so-called voyaging sailboats.

Does that mean bigger is better? Well, if one had unlimited funds, I suppose you cannot dispute that bigger is more comfortable. If my own financial situation allowed it, I would be on a never-ending trade winds circumnavigation as skipper of a 90-footer, crewed by former Dallas Cowboys cheerleaders, and flying home only to see my family and pick up boat parts.

But given that most of us are not blessed with unlimited cruising kitties, I would encourage you to start by looking as objectively as possible at the minimums and maximums of what you would like from your potential purchase. By that I mean what are you sure you will do regularly with your sailboat, and what is the possible larger task that may lie ahead. Below are some of the questions you need to ask.

Am I Coastal Cruising or Crossing Oceans?

There is a big difference in expense and preparation for a cruise to the Bahamas or to Baja Mexico versus a circumnavigation. Granted some people will still purchase a windvane self-steering system and watermaker even if they are not really necessary, but the bottom line is you can save yourself thousands of dollars by being honest with yourself (and your significant other) before you depart.

There is nothing wrong with starting out coastal cruising as a test and then, if interest and funds allow, doing any necessary final upgrades or even switching to a different boat. After all, if you are coastal cruising, you should never be more than a thousand miles from a major port that will allow you to finalize your new plans.

Do the Cruising Areas I Want to Visit Have Mostly Marinas or Anchorages?

For better or worse, cruising is getting more popular every decade. There are rallies you can join, for a fee, that will nursemaid you around the world, with a mechanic or a doctor never too far away from VHF contact. It is now also possible to circumnavigate and stay in marinas at all the major ports or cruising grounds you visit. And not just a dock with cleats and a water hose, but purpose-built facilities that have power, potable water, and wi-fi. Even if you prefer to anchor out, some areas are now either forbidding the use of anchors and requiring the rental of moorings, or even charging just for the privilege of putting down your own hook. In my own stomping grounds of Cabo San Lucas, Mexico, a launch will come out to your anchorage within a few hours and collect, as of this writing, about five dollars per day.

Since the majority of these marinas are optimized for 40- to 50-foot fiberglass monohulls, it is worth keeping this in mind before you buy a multihull or a bargain wooden boat that either will not fit in the marina slips you may visit or will not be allowed in the first place. Yes, that's right, a number of newer marinas do not allow wooden or ferro-cement boats. Some will not allow vessels more than 30 years old *no matter what the construction.* Call it age discrimination or whatever you want, but there is no bill of rights to protect your 40-year-old classic—no matter how much she gleams—if a marina manager (or an insurance company) has decided they want only newer boats.

So if you think you will have the budget and desire to use marinas on a regular basis, keep in mind that a monohull up to

---

WEB RESOURCES FOR CRUISING SAILBOATS

www.sailboatdata.com Great starting point for finding out basic dimensions on most sailboats that had significant production runs. Line drawings and layouts shown for many models, plus sometimes links to other useful sites for specific models.

www.cruisersforum.com Has a multitude of interesting threads that you can search to find out about boats in general, cruising, and specific systems on boats. Or you can start a thread of your own. If you need to know where you can find new injectors for a 30-year-old Saab diesel, an amazing array of experts or owners are ready to come back with help.

www.sailnet.com Takes a bulletin board approach, with categories for pretty much everything. Focuses a little more on sailing gear and commercial outlets, but can be useful for a lot of items, even finding crew. Has a bit of an East Coast bias.

www.sailboatowners.com Has a lot of owners groups using its platform, and is easy to search for any thread that may be useful for your specific need or question.

www.cruisingworld.com A very slickly done portal from the well-known cruising magazine with some quality blogs from cruisers like Alvah Simon and Herb McCormick. Also has boat reviews, although they are restricted.

www.goodoldboat.com The title says it all, though the site does not appear to run a forum, and it charges to download past issues.

www.cruiser.co.za/links1.asp A great assembly of links to quality blogs and websites of serious cruisers, especially circumnavigators and boats that have been out many years.

www.sailblogs.com An unfiltered portal that takes all comers. A bit difficult to find the serious cruisers, but there are some available on this platform.

www.bluewaterboats.org Has a Wiki approach to reviews with various contributors. The database is growing daily with everything from light reviews to some excellent in-depth treatments.

www.spinsheet.com/used-boat-reviews This has what appears to be a collection of Jack Hornor's sailboat reviews over the past years, with nice introductions into models not discussed in this book.

www.ssca.org The Seven Seas Cruising Association was founded in 1952 by six couples in California and is the most popular membership organization for cruisers. Most are pretty serious sailors, and although their forums have less traffic, the quality is often quite good. You can use the forums without becoming a paying member.

www.oceannavigator.com A serious site for serious sailors. Plenty of no-cost educational articles and other stuff to whet the appetite.

www.bwsailing.com Blue Water Sailing tends to focus more on new boats and products due to a need for advertising revenue. Not a lot of free content available.

www.sailmagazine.com There was a time when I could not wait for my issue of *Sail* to arrive. Herb Payson's articles in the 1970s first got me hooked on cruising. Unfortunately most content now is pretty mainstream due to a need to cater to the charter companies and the new boat manufacturers in order to pay the bills.

50 feet will have the easiest time getting a slip.

These are just some of the initial questions. Other issues to consider are how many people will you regularly be sleeping on board? What is the largest sail you are comfortable furling or reefing by yourself? What is the largest boat you are comfortable docking?

Much will depend, of course, on your own experience base, or lack thereof. If you have never cruised, and you admire the cavernous V-berth on a boat you are considering buying, who is going to be there to tell you that V-berths are almost useless for sleeping on passages? Or that the hull-to-deck joint on the design you like has had problems for much of its production run?

There is a lot to be said for those who know what they don't know, and can resist the temptation to buy the first dock queen that strikes their fancy. This doesn't mean that you can't be smitten by the comely curves of a particular boat; it just means that you then have to have the sense to

start digging to find out more about it. I believe that in the legal profession, it is called due diligence.

Fortunately with the advent of the Internet, it is easier than ever to research opinions and facts about cruising sailboats. The accompanying sidebar Web Resources for Cruising Sailboats lists some of the better websites.

Of course besides Internet options, there is also that quaint, almost obsolete item known as the book. My goal here is not to rehash information that is already out there in some very detailed books. (References and Further Reading, on page 161, contains some excellent choices.) I especially recommend you check out offerings from Beth Leonard, Charles Doane, Jim Howard, and Nigel Calder. Doane's tome *The Modern Cruising Sailboat* is as close as you will get to a bible for cruising wannabes, and is required reading.

Once you have performed some due diligence, you can fire up the laptop and get serious about finding your ticket to ride.

The Search Begins

That's what a ship is, you know—it's not just a keel and a hull and a deck and sails. That's what a ship needs. But what a ship is, really is, is freedom.

—CAPTAIN JACK SPARROW

How Not to Buy a Boat

There is nothing rational about boats or cruising. If you dream about anchoring in front of swaying palms on a tropical bay, in most cases it would be cheaper to fly there first class and stay in the best local hotel. The actual purchase of a boat, then, is usually a very emotional and often impulsive decision. You are buying into a lifestyle, one of the last truly free areas of adventure, but in a wet and rolling cocoon moving at a speed that most 4-year-olds can beat at a jog. So what follows is how NOT to buy a boat.

Do not buy a big cruising boat if you have never sailed, even if you have subscribed to sailing magazines for thirty years. Try a charter first, or at least do some sailing with some friends, or crew on a boat making a significant passage in line with your aspirations.

Do not buy a boat based solely on its lines, no matter how sexy she may look. This rule can also be applied to marriages, but that discussion is for another time and place.

Do not buy a boat just because the price is incredibly low. There is usually a good reason the price is low, and unless you know how to change out engines, replace keel bolts, or strip gelcoat with a grinder, you may find that sometimes cheap is not really cheap.

Do not buy any wooden boat or a fiberglass boat over 30 years old if you plan to use marinas a lot. Many marinas will not even take vessels like this, or the cost to insure them will be higher if the marina places different requirements on your boat.

Do not buy a boat within 24 hours of receiving an unexpected windfall.

Do not buy a boat just because you think it will help you with the opposite sex.

And finally, do not buy a boat without a survey—unless you are a boatbuilder or a surveyor yourself. I have been a surveyor for much of my career, but even I hire a surveyor for a personal yacht purchase since they almost always spot something important that I might have missed, especially if I have already presold myself on the design and might be wearing my "rose-colored sunglasses." Of course it is important to find the right surveyor. Many specialize in certain types of yachts. You need to know their focus beforehand.

Where to Search for the Best Price

Having made these points, we can now turn to the physical search for your cruising boat. Remember that it is not my goal here to revisit all the parameters that make for a good cruising sailboat. There are plenty of good books already out there for that. Instead we are offering up twenty potential candidates (and one Honorable Mention) and reviewing them. None of them is perfect, but all have been used for bluewater voyages with success. And all are available for less than $50,000. So whether you choose one within these pages or are open to other designs, let's now look at how to find a cruising sailboat at the best possible price.

Internet Search Engines

It would be hard to argue that the Internet is the most powerful tool to come along in the last forty years. If I wake up in the middle of the night with a sudden urge to buy a Swan 37, I can easily boot up my laptop, plug in my price and location limits in a search engine like YachtWorld, and less than a minute later be looking at a picture of the nav station on a Swan 37, for sale somewhere in Finland.

In North America the website Yacht-World.com is the dominant search engine for finding brokered sailboats. Only bona fide yacht brokers can list on this service, and with smart early marketing this website quickly cornered the market for brokered boat listings. Individuals cannot list here, and there are a few options for them on other sites, but if your boat has a value of at least $25,000, the odds are it will be on Yachtworld.com. So let's look at how to best use the site.

If you are already presold on a specific design, you can use the advanced search feature (seen on the YachtWorld home page at column left) to specify the exact manufacturer and model you want to find. But I would usually recommend a more general search, bearing in mind that if you are on a budget, it probably does not make sense to search listings on the East Coast if you are based on the West Coast. This is not always the case—I have seen some couples decide to start their cruise on the coast opposite the one they intended because they got a deal on a boat that was too good to pass up—but in general you want to stick with Left Coast or Right.

But here is the key—do not be tempted by all the prompts to use too many filters in your search. Use only the fewest filters possible, or too many good listings may slip through and never be seen.

For instance, if a broker is sloppy in setting up his YachtWorld listing, he may omit some data on his client's boat that could negatively affect your search. Or sometimes the broker does a quick preliminary listing just to get something online but without photos or all the correct details. He may not specify that it has a diesel engine because he forgot to enter it, which means that if you are searching only for boats with diesel engines, that listing may not come up.

So it is better for you to use as few filters as possible. When I do YachtWorld searches as a surveyor and I need to get comps for establishing market value, I am very specific. But when I am searching for possible cruising boats for myself or a client, I usually put in only boat length, price range, location, and hull material (fiberglass). After all, even if you end up

THE INTERNET—A BLESSING AND A CURSE

Along with the over-hyped boats, there also exist the over-criticized boats. And no more powerful tool has ever been created for criticism than the Internet. Whole industries have popped up to defend reputations, and still others to dissect every aspect of, well, everything. Including boats.

So when you see me (lovingly) refer to "forum rats" in this book, I am simply poking a little fun at individuals tucked behind their laptops who are dismissive of a boat design they have never seen just because it has a spade rudder. Or a sloop rig instead of a cutter rig. Or a fiberglass hull instead of a steel one.

I have learned to keep my jump-to-conclusions in check. Once I was anchored in a popular Mexican port with about nine other boats, all of them slick fiberglass models recently out of San Diego. They sported custom radar arches, shiny new dinghies, solar panels, and the like. But tucked away in a far corner of the bay was a beat-up double-ender built of ferro-cement, her topsides streaked with rust stains. That boat had just completed a circumnavigation and had all the other yachts beat by about 30,000 nautical miles.

It is fine to have your biases, especially those built on personal experience. But with the advent of the Internet, a prospective cruiser has a powerful tool at his or her disposal—not just for affirmation of their boat choice but plenty of strangers ready to tear it down. On many occasions I have seen a wannabe open a new thread on a forum by saying they are "thinking about buying" a given design and then asking for opinions. Dozens of instant experts will then chime in, explaining why their own boats are better or why the inquirer is crazy to even think about setting sail in such an inappropriate boat. And how many of the respondents actually own or have sea time in the design being discussed? Usually precious few.

If you are truly on a budget, the thing to remember is this—what others see as a deal killer may for you be a deal maker. Why? Because the "deal killer" will act to lower the price on a boat that is otherwise a good candidate for you as a cruiser. Recently I saw an early Cal 39 that had a newer diesel and excellent sails and electronics, and could be had for under $30,000. Why so cheap? The boat had tiller steering, which is out of fashion.

There are, of course, some things that you should probably not budge on. Don't accept an old gas engine instead of a diesel, for instance. But if you really want to find a deal, then you may want to be ready to compromise on things like tiller versus wheel, or aft cockpit when you perhaps want a center cockpit.

(continued next page)

THE INTERNET—A BLESSING AND A CURSE, *CONTINUED*

The forum rats out there may sniff their noses at your spade rudder or the lack of a swim step transom, but if you are out there doing it while they are on their butts dreaming about it (or preaching online about how to do it right), then you get the last laugh.

There is one final aspect of the Internet to keep in mind, and unfortunately I speak from personal experience. Within a few seconds one can put in some search parameters and be looking at boats thousands of miles away, right down to a detailed equipment list. The Internet wipes away the distance between you and that Island Palms 35 you have been lusting for. There it is, in beautiful, albeit small, digital photos for you to peruse.

A few years ago I had some money in the bank and was killing time on YachtWorld when I came across a 43-foot design that had always intrigued me. The nice little photos seemed fine, the price was great, and soon I was on the phone to the broker. The boat was in Florida and I was in California, but I knew I could get it trucked out for about $5,000 if I was not in a rush. The broker assured me that the boat was in great shape. A few more minutes on the Internet and I had my plane ticket printed out.

When I finally made it to the private dock about four days later and went below into the boat's saloon, there was obvious water damage on most of the vertical teak veneers. Leaking ports had caused the wood to swell and crack to the point where thousands of dollars of work would be needed to remedy the problem. I knew in about ten seconds that the deal was off. When I asked the broker why none of his thirty pictures taken for the listing showed the damage (or why he did not at least mention it knowing I was flying three thousand miles to see the boat) he mumbled something about it being only a "cosmetic" issue.

So before you pick up that mouse, remember that the Internet increases the temptation at the same time it increases the convenience of shopping for boats.

with fifty to a hundred possibilities, it does not take long to scan through and pull out the most interesting candidates. Shopping is often the most enjoyable part of the process. You haven't had to start writing checks yet!

In some cases sellers don't want to use a broker, and if you have cash you can find some deals this way. Good websites include www.sailboatlistings.com, www.craigslist.org, and sometimes www.ebay.com. (See the list of websites in Chapter Two.) If you are interested in an eBay listing, you need to be very careful in any bidding situation to avoid a legal obligation on a boat that you may not have seen, much less surveyed. I would never recommend buying an eBay boat sight unseen, no matter how much experience you may feel you bring to the table. In my experience, sailboats on eBay rarely sell on the first try anyway, and are sometimes in a permanent state of auction, trolling for a buyer. So there is rarely as much time pressure as the seller may want you to believe. Treat an eBay lead as just that—a lead. If you are within a day's drive and like the photos you have seen, *maybe* it is worth pursuing.

Private ad listings on places like craigslist or sailboatlistings.com carry the usual caveats. It always amazes me when I hear stories about how some otherwise intelligent people have been suckered out of a 10 percent deposit on a boat by a scam artist. One scenario is a guy who has discovered where the boat key is located (do we *always* need to put them in a cockpit locker or a coaming box?) and then takes a picture and runs it in an online ad at a great price. The meeting is at the marina, so no home address is needed. Billy the Buyer shows up, watches the guy locate the key and open the boat, and loves what he sees. Sammy the Scammer says he has two other interested parties but will hold the boat with a 10 percent deposit, and will bring the title and paperwork to their next meeting to settle everything. Guess who ends up out several thousand dollars in this ruse? What are the odds that the real boatowner will show up during the half hour it takes to pull this off? Slim to none.

In-Person Searching

Walking the docks of local marinas may be the best way of all to find a deal on a cruiser. Many boats may not be listed but really are for sale; the owner just does not realize it yet. He or she is reluctant to let go of that cruising dream. If you see a boat with a huge organic farm hanging off the bottom and an inch of dirt covering the cabintop, you may have found a candidate for purchase, as long as it can still be brought back into shape.

The trick will be to obtain the contact information of the owner. My own experience has been to walk the docks on weekends when neighboring boaters may be around, and try to find out how to reach an owner. If the boat is documented with the U.S. Coast Guard, write down the info, and when you get home you can simply go to the USCG National Vessel Documentation Center home page and perform a search by the boat name and home port of the boat that has caught your eye.

Another tactic is to buddy up to the marina office personnel and tell them you

are trying to reach an owner about buying his boat. Of course they will not release the contact info to you, but sometimes they can be persuaded to contact him or her on your behalf to relay your interest. Just make sure you don't say anything about moving the prospective boat to another marina or long-term boatyard or they will clam up fast, not wanting to lose a tenant.

Marina employees can often help you narrow down some choices if you ask the right questions. They will know if someone has been slow to pay slip fees, or maybe if the boat has not left the slip for years, and might be surprisingly forthcoming if they think you are a good credit risk to take over the slip obligations.

If you do finally reach the owner of that long-neglected gem in the rough, you need to be delicate in your approach. As I said before, many boats are for sale; the owner just hasn't figured it out yet. You can't just shatter his or her cruising dreams completely from the start. Here are some possible approaches, bad and good:

"Hi, thanks for taking my call. I guess you own the Pipe Dream. *Look, buddy, the marina says you haven't taken the boat out since the Carter administration, and the boat sure looks that way. I think we both know you're never going cruising, so why not let someone buy her cheap and live out your dream for you?"*

That was a bad approach. Better might be something like this:

"Hi, thanks for taking my call. I saw the Pipe Dream *and, boy, that is a design I've always admired. I'm really trying to get out there cruising and have a limited budget, but I do have some cash, and I'd love to talk to you about giving me a chance to fix her up and take her sailing.*

Can I buy you a coffee this weekend down at the marina restaurant?"

Another tip. If the boat is owned by a husband but his wife answers the phone, make sure she finds out that you are calling to inquire about buying the boat. Odds are that she is tired of watching it suck up money without going anywhere. One time that I did this, the husband told me he was not interested in selling. He called me back the next day. His wife told him to get real and start negotiating!

Other Types of Sales

Marina lien sales are sometimes described as good options for finding a cruising boat, but I have never seen anything but small boats in this type of sale. Once in a while you might see a 32-footer come along, but even if you can buy the boat for almost nothing, it will make little sense if the engine is seized, the fuel tanks are corroded, the rigging is suspect, etc. In most cases, unless you are very handy and know how to source what you will need for the refit, the lien sales will not help you much.

If you do want to check these possibilities, call the larger marinas directly to see when their next lien sale will occur, or monitor the classifieds of the local boating trade magazines.

Repo brokers and liquidation specialists have come along since the Great Recession began, with an occasional sailboat bargain to be found among what are usually powerboat repossessions. These sources are not traditional yacht brokers, although they may have obtained a broker's license for marketing purposes. Many of them do not really know anything about the boats they are selling, and the boat may be a long distance away from their base. It is rare to find anything other than

a bare-bones sailboat via these outlets.

In some cases the boat will be a salvage sale after the boat was in a fire or sank. I would never, ever take on a boat that was salvaged after a fire or a sinking. The most I would consider would be a hull-damaged boat (such as post-hurricane), and even then only if it had passed a survey for structural integrity.

Of all the above options, I have had the most success with being quick and ready on YachtWorld and buying through a conventional broker. That process will be treated in the next chapter. But before we get there, let's look at what your minimum standards should be as to overall condition, and then the equipment list you are looking for on your would-be cruiser.

The Fixer-Upper Conundrum

One of the hardest things to determine, assuming you are handy around boats, is when to buy a fixer-upper with an attractive price and lots of potential. The price can be so low that the temptation is enormous, but even if you have extensive boat maintenance skills, you need to take a chill pill and make sure that what you are about to do makes sense. I speak from experience, unfortunately, having on at least one occasion bitten off more boat project than I could chew—and suffering the consequences.

In many areas of the country, the only place you can do major work on your boat is at a boatyard, some of which do not even allow do-it-yourself labor because they have to comply with strict environmental regulations. Most marinas will not let you overhaul the diesel, paint the hull, or re-rig the mast at the slip. Found a great bargain boat but it has blisters and you want to grind off the gelcoat? Make sure you have a cheap and legal place to do the work. *So even if you have the skill set to effect the renovations your boat needs, make sure you have a place to do it.*

There is plenty of literature out there to take you deeper into the selection process and even how you should plan any potential renovation of a used sailboat. But by far the best required reading is Don Casey's *This Old Boat* (see References and Further Reading). Don starts out with an interesting requirement for any boat you may buy—beauty. Or at least beauty in the eye of the most important beholder— you:

"I lead the list with beauty because, for most of us, boating—sailing in particular—fills some kind of aesthetic need. There is nothing pragmatic about pleasure boating; it is entirely a romantic endeavor. If the sight of the boat you are considering does not quicken your pulse, she will ultimately prove unsatisfactory no matter how seaworthy, commodious, or practical."

Truer words have never been written. In researching this book, it was amazing how quickly I received pictures of the personal sailboat of any individual I would write to when asking for input and quality photos. So make sure the lines of whatever you are looking at set your little heart aflutter. It will make the time pass more quickly when you start refinishing those decks or rebuilding the engine!

I have stumbled across good websites, including http://www.billdietrich.me/Costs.html#Refitting, that have some excellent pages regarding refit projects and their pitfalls. But the best list I have seen of what might be involved in refitting an older boat can be found in Beth Leonard's *The Voyager's Handbook*.

Refit Costs: Some Rough Figures

(Reprinted with permission of Beth Leonard from *The Voyager's Handbook*.)

The following list will give you a rough idea of what it can cost to upgrade the basic structure and systems on a 20- to 30-year-old 40-foot boat to a level appropriate for offshore sailing and living. The labor-hour estimates are for professional labor experienced at the specific task with no complications in the project.

Replace spars and standing rigging: $15,000 plus 40 labor-hours

Rebuild bow platform, add electric windlass: $3,000 plus 40 labor-hours

Replace hatches/ports: $500–$1,000 plus 8 labor-hours per opening

Replace engine, transmission, prop shaft, propeller: $15,000 plus 80–100 labor-hours

Rewire entire boat, replace all lights, replace electrical boxes and all fuses: $2,500 plus 80–100 labor-hours

Replace all hoses, plumbing fittings, seacocks, and through-hulls: $2,500 plus 80–100 labor-hours

Replace toilet and sanitation hoses, install holding tank: $1,000 plus 20 labor-hours

Install propane stove, propane tanks, and propane locker: $2,000 plus 20 labor-hours

Replace all cushions throughout boat: $500 plus 40 labor-hours

The above are Leonard's estimates for just renewing the basic boat systems and don't even consider the costs of added equipment or upgrades. The lesson here is that some projects are so big and potentially expensive that it is senseless to take them on in the first place, especially given that there are plenty of used boat options out there.

Here are some of the projects you want to avoid in buying your cruising boat, and others that may not be a deal breaker as long as you have the skills to undertake the work.

Big Projects to Avoid

Complete re-rigging, repowering (unless you are very mechanically inclined, and access is excellent), rewiring, multiple tank replacements, complete sail inventory replacement, major blisters, gelcoat crazing, frame/bulkhead attachment issues, keel joint issues, complete canvas overhaul, bottom paint spalling (adhesion failure), warped or heavily worn cabin sole, multiple hatches or ports that need replacing, teak decks ready for replacing.

Projects That Can Be Considered

Cosmetic painting or varnishing, old electronics in need of updating, one tank that needs replacing, one sail that needs replacing or repair, some canvas that needs replacement or repair, bottom paint ready for renewal, mast that needs painting, teak and holly sole that needs refinishing, one hatch or port that needs replacing or rebedding, running rigging that needs replacing.

This is a generalized list and does not consider some of the nuances of your decision. For instance, it has never been important to me to have self-tailing winches, so I never considered the very significant cost to upgrade an older sailboat from conventional winches to self-tailers. But if self-tailers are important to you, then do your best to find a boat that already has them installed. Otherwise, you are looking at maybe six months of cruising funds just to put in the winches you want.

Another nuance is topside painting versus repainting decks, cockpit, and cabin sides. It is actually fairly easy to paint topsides on a typical sailboat; it is the largest area to paint but is also uncluttered by fixtures and hardware. The rest of the boat, however, is littered with fittings, ports, tracks, and whatever particular nonskid finish was used when building the boat. This sort of paint job is much more difficult, involving a lot more masking and detail work. So for my part I don't shy away from a boat needing the topsides refinished, as long as the rest of the gelcoat or paint is still serviceable.

Finally, there are a lot of deals out there on boats that need engines replaced or rebuilt. If the physical access is reasonable and the price reflects the value of the engine, it is not really that difficult for someone mechanically inclined to replace a small diesel. Obviously if you are not mechanically inclined, you are looking at sky-high hourly labor rates to have specialists do the work for you, so contemplate this option only if you have no doubt that you can handle the work. I have done this several times with great success, usually calling around to independent diesel mechanics who have a sideline business rebuilding diesels that they have pulled out for customers at no cost to the mechanic. Then I have bought excellent rebuilt engines, sometimes with a 90-day warranty, at half the price of new. The Yanmar GM series is especially good for this sort of approach.

Essential Equipment for Bluewater Sailing

Assuming you have found some candidates for purchase that have the lines and the basic systems you are looking for, it may

Peter Powell's Mwelu *in Los Cabos, Mexico, after voyaging from Rhode Island through the Panama Canal. Peter said what he liked best about the boat—a Hunter 37—is that Cherubini designed it as a true cutter rather than working backward from a sloop rig.*

be Equipment Lists that will really make for significant differences between any finalists in your Goldilocks cruiser competition. But just what is essential to have and what is only desirable? Much of this will depend upon your own skill level in installing any desired gear that is already on the boat, for instance:

Below-decks autopilots are always high on my desired equipment list. Since they are expensive to purchase and install, and since they make the difference between pleasure and pain on even a coastal cruise, my last two boats had these already installed when I bought them. It is at least $5,000 in savings to have one already installed as opposed to buying and installing one using a pro. It is worth noting, however, that both of the two boats I sea trialed that had below-deck pilots

failed the sea trial when the units failed to perform—unless you call steering the boat in a constant circle to starboard "performing." So make sure you verify their function. If the autopilot is working but is an antique, bear in mind that service once you are out there will be more than problematic, and autopilots do fail. Personally I like only Robertson and Alpha autopilots. Navico, Autohelm, and Wagner autopilots are somewhat less preferable.

Windvanes are similar in this regard. If you really will be going bluewater cruising, it will save you thousands if the boat already has a windvane. However, it is fairly rare to find a cruiser already vane-equipped since most coastal cruisers opt for autopilots. So don't make it a deal breaker, or more of a dealmaker in case of a tie. If you look a little, windvanes can

PRIORITY EQUIPMENT

Assuming you have a strong hull and rig, anchors, normal sails (with or without furling), and a diesel engine, here is what I consider to be priority equipment for offshore sailing. My order of priority of course will not agree with everyone's.

- Manual and electric bilge pumps
- Compass and depthsounder
- GPS with chartplotter, minimum 6-inch screen
- VHF radio with AIS (automatic identification system)
- Sturdy dinghy, hard or soft
- Dodger and bimini
- Autopilot, preferably below-decks
- Windlass, preferably electric
- Dedicated stormsail(s)
- Inverter
- Radar, preferably integrated with AIS
- Removable inner forestay with staysail
- Solar panels or extra battery bank
- SSB (single-sideband modulation) or satellite texting capability
- Windvane or backup autopilot
- Watermaker
- Emergency rudder (unless windvane equipped)
- Backup dinghy or kayak
- Feathering prop
- Wind generator

breaking waves on a barrier reef will usually show up on radar, as will rainsqualls, and especially a BOSS (big oncoming steel ship). But radar is actually not as difficult to install as an autopilot, in my opinion, and can be purchased for under two thousand dollars, so if the boat does not have radar, I would use its absence only as a bargaining chip if the price is still not where you need it.

Watermakers are a big-ticket item occasionally included, but make sure they have either been getting used regularly or have been "pickled" for a layup period. Otherwise the membrane will need replacing, and this can cost an easy grand. Can you cruise without a watermaker? Of course, but if you don't have big water tanks, be prepared for plenty of schlepping jerry jugs in 90 degree temperatures to slowly pour sometimes questionable water into your tanks. Either that, or learn to shower using a quart of water. Watermakers consume a lot of power, so remember that when you want to make water, you will need to run the engine or a small generator.

Refrigeration is also nice, but in some ways I would rather go without refrigeration than not have a watermaker. This is because having refrigeration sets off a chain reaction as to high electrical demands. You will need to run the engine fairly regularly (or have a genset), and have excellent battery capacity, and maintain the refrigeration system itself. Although my last few boats have had refrigeration, in my earlier low-budget days I did fine without it. Of course, I am also okay living on tuna fish or peanut butter sandwiches. Remember, too, that much of the food in the developing world is packaged with the idea that refrigeration may not be avail-

often be found on the Internet for sale by returning cruisers. On the West Coast you can always find them at Minney's Surplus in Newport Beach at 50 percent less than new.

Radar is certainly not indispensable if you are on a tight budget and will be cruising the tropics, but it is becoming rare to see a cruising boat without one. The able. So in Mexico and farther south, it is very easy to buy milk that can be stored at room temperature until opened.

Dodgers can be very pricey, so as mentioned it is desirable to have at least a salvageable dodger frame to begin with. This way even if the fabric is rotted, you will not have to start from scratch.

Biminis may not be present if you are looking at boats in temperate climes, but at least they are not as expensive to install as dodgers, and it may even be possible to use an off-the-shelf model.

Chartplotters and GPS units are usually present on any boat these days, but if for some reason they are missing, outdated, or broken, they are very easy to install. As far as I am concerned, having a good depthsounder installed and working is more important than any GPS installation issue. A GPS antenna is typically installed at deck level in the cockpit and is no major job. Many of the newer units don't even require a remotely mounted antenna.

Dinghies and outboards are always nice to see on the equipment list. Of course installation is not a factor here, but if the boat is big enough for davits and you want them, you will be thousands of dollars ahead if you can find a cruiser that already has them.

Windlasses and ground tackle are important, especially if you are sold on an

BOATBUILDING STANDARDS AND OFFSHORE PRODUCTION

For the sailors who would prefer to write a check for a boat rather than spend five years of weekends finishing it on their own, a shift to offshore production provided a huge boon. In the 1970s yacht designers and entrepreneurs were discovering that they could fly to Taiwan (in those days called Formosa) and get a custom-built yacht for half of what it would cost them in the United States. The interior joinerwork was often superior to that on U.S. production boats, and these "Taiwan Teakies" had the salty look that the market was begging for amongst generally conservative American sailors.

John Edwards of Hans Christian Yachts (in Taiwan) was at the forefront of the 1970s switch to Taiwanese boatbuilders, but he was smart enough to realize that a good Scandinavian name was far better for his new brand, just as Haagen Dazs ice cream is not made in Denmark but New York. The Hans Christian line was produced in Taiwan. It is amazing just how far this marketing gimmick can take you.

I have met serious boat buyers who assure me that Nordhavn powerboats are made in Sweden (they are made in China) and that the Hans Christian 38 was made in Denmark—the home of Hans Christian Andersen! According to yacht designer Robert Perry, the running joke was "High in the Alps of Taiwan is a small German village where they build Hans Christian yachts." And so, dear reader, if I have to be the one to tell you that boats with names like Norseman, Lafitte, or Monte Fino were actually built in Asia, I am sorry.

Since several Taiwan-built designs are included on The List herein, it is worthwhile to take a cross-cultural look at boatbuilding standards. Few government-mandated boatbuilding standards exist in Taiwan or North America—at least for recreational vessels. I start with U.S. industry requirements and then provide a few anecdotal stories regarding the lax atmosphere seen in the Far East.

In the United States, surveyors like myself will often refer to the *(continued next page)*

BOATBUILDING STANDARDS AND OFFSHORE PRODUCTION, *CONTINUED*

Code of Federal Regulations (CFRs) on our survey reports. These are, in fact, requirements and not the voluntary standards described later. But in reality most of the CFR requirements apply to gasoline-powered boats under twenty feet since that was the typical recreational vessel at the time that most of the code was written.

The CFRs referred to on most surveys deal only with safety equipment such as flares and extinguishers, or having the ship's batteries properly strapped down, or perhaps the proper posting of pollution regulations. There are almost no structural standards described for larger recreational boats, although for inspected vessels (for instance, a boat that carries passengers) there is a more stringent level of compliance, and an actual physical inspection usually takes place. As for recreational boats, the government has largely let the industry police itself using voluntary guidelines set by private organizations like the American Boat and Yacht Council (ABYC).

The ABYC was started in the 1950s as an attempt to finally bring, albeit gradually, some objective yacht construction and repair standards to the marine industry. Eventually, over sixty-five standards, involving everything from correct sizing for electrical wiring to proper propane storage, would be developed. Some were considered mandatory while others were suggested. The more established and responsible American manufacturers adopted most of the ABYC proposals.

In addition to the ABYC, perhaps the more dominant trade organization in North American boatbuilding is the National Marine Manufacturers Association (NMMA). NMMA was first a promotional organization that included the sponsorship of the popular annual International BoatBuilders' Exhibition and Conference (IBEX), but it has been increasingly more involved over the years in establishing manufacturing standards.

Rather than reinvent the wheel, NMMA has worked in conjunction with the ABYC to incorporate most of their detailed standards into a certification process, allowing compliant boatbuilders to affix a "NMMA Certified" placard to their hulls. Individual components that comply with applicable standards can also be labeled as certified in a system similar to the well-known Underwriters Laboratories ("UL Listed") consumer product program.

So perhaps as the federal government intended, there exists a baseline level of mandated construction standards and required safety gear (under the CFRs) but also a much more detailed standard level that the industry has developed with the ABYC and NMMA. Just remember that NMMA certification was not widely used when the boats described in this book were being built, and that compliance is voluntary. Only the Code of Federal Regulations carries the weight of law.

Far East Observations

Taiwan, alas, has no such tradition of standards or certifications. Some boatbuilders may voluntarily comply—or profess to comply—with standards such as ABYC or the International Standards Organization (ISO), but I can state from personal experience that Taiwan yards vary greatly in quality. Beginning in the 1990s, I flew to Taiwan on behalf of clients having powerboats built there, and I later owned a Formosa 43 of my own (a variation of the Ron Holland 43).

Most of my experience has been in the Kaohsiung area, which has traditionally been a booming area for yacht construction (more recently some companies have opened yards in mainland China or Malaysia, where labor prices are cheaper). While most of the U.S. brands that started building their boats in Taiwan in the 1970s were well intentioned, the distance and cultural barriers involved were and are huge.

North American dealers or even company owners who tried to provide their own internal inspection process by flying across the Pacific every three months were often frustrated. I saw that it was pretty easy for Taiwan yard bosses to pay only lip service to the detailed "requirements" of their American patrons. Most of them had the attitude that they had been building boats for years and knew what they were doing, and they were slow to adopt new industry practices, especially if it meant added cost to a set build price. Once the three-day fly-in was over and the Americans or Canadians were back on their return flight, very little changed.

Taiwan boatbuilding is strongest in areas that are labor intensive, such as woodworking, and weakest in materials technology that involves quality control. At the risk of oversimplifying things, a typical Taiwan boat might boast beautiful detailed teak cabinetry replete with arched doors and dozens of dovetail joints, but also incorporate plywood that does not have marine-grade glues or wiring that was not tinned and therefore much more prone to corrosion. [I sold marine hardware for a time, and learned firsthand that it was not unusual for a Taiwan foundry to take a common piece of U.S. hardware, such as a Merriman or Perko cleat, and then sand-cast it out of bronze or stainless steel. But there is stainless and then there is stainless, with the U.S. manufacturers adhering to some semblance of quality control and the Taiwanese (or Korean) often stamping their wire rope spools as 316 stainless when, in fact, it falls short. It was not uncommon for

me to magnet-test supposedly stainless steel rigging wire in Taiwan and find it lacking. Or find that it was "tiger-striped" before it was even installed due to the die used for wrapping not being properly cleaned.]

On the more expensive yachts, ex-pat Brits and Aussies were making a living personally supervising the construction of their client's boats for a percentage of the overall cost. In many cases it was money well spent.

But for mass-produced sailboats, there just wasn't that sort of oversight. If the item included on a boat, such as a mast or an engine, came directly from a respected manufacturer, then you were subject only to the vagaries of the Taiwanese installation process. But the less easily checked sundries, such as stainless or bronze fittings, wiring, and plumbing, were often the areas that suffered.

One of the most common places to cut corners was keel construction. Ever notice how almost all Taiwan boats use encapsulated keels? True, most are cruising designs, but even when a designer stipulated that all ballast be lead, or better yet external lead, the yard owner often talked the American or Canadian company involved out of it. Even at Ta Yang, a more respected builder, the Tayana 37 ballast was typically iron and not lead. And in some cases at lesser yards, anything from steel punchings to an old typewriter may have been used, all conveniently hidden under a slurry of resin or cement.

While much of this was due to cost, another reason for the encapsulated keels was the shipping process. Sailboats had to be loaded aboard a ship as deck cargo for a long transpacific voyage. Ideally they were set in custom cradles that distributed the boat's weight properly, but often the keel had to take most of the weight and some knocking around. External lead *(continued next page)*

BOATBUILDING STANDARDS AND OFFSHORE PRODUCTION, *CONTINUED*

keels were more delicate and required cautious handling, plus some possible cosmetic repairs once they reached North America.

This may seem like a blanket condemnation of Taiwanese boats. But I have happily owned one and just wanted to emphasize the following: reputations are important in North American boatbuilding—and even more so in Asian boatbuilding. Since there are very few mandatory standards or inspections, you need to treat every boat as an individual and, yes, use a surveyor unless you are yourself vastly experienced. Pay particular attention to chainplates, tanks, wiring, plumbing, stainless rigging, and anything that is a "knockoff"

of an originally U.S. part or system. Virtually every North American marine hardware item, from anchors to steering systems, has been duplicated in some back-alley foundry overseas. I have seen it with my own eyes.

The big change in the Far East today is that Taiwanese labor rates, once considered quite cheap, are now considered too expensive: As mentioned, many builders have moved to mainland China, Malaysia, and elsewhere. Boatbuilders are abandoning an island that, despite not having the most consistent or verifiable building methods, had still created generations of skilled artisans, particularly in woodworking.

---

electric unit. In some ways electric windlasses are a safety issue because I know that I am much more likely to raise the hook and reanchor in a sketchy situation if all I have to do is push a button. If I'm ashore, I might get lazy and convince myself that staying put will work out. My last three boats had electric windlasses, two of them installed myself after purchase. If you are in your bunk and the wind shifts at night and you have a manual windlass, you may hesitate. But with an electric unit, you will usually get out on deck and make the move.

Sail inventory is also important because new sails have gotten so incredibly expensive. In fact, having a complete suit of sails built for a used 32-footer can often exceed the value of the boat itself. So my rule is that I am willing to consider replacing a worn-out mainsail, or add a drifter that is lacking, but I avoid buying a boat that needs two or more new sails.

Solar panels are ubiquitous on cruis-

ers these days. If they're not on the equipment list, you should at least have an idea as to where they could be mounted. If you are looking at a double-ender and want solar panels, remember that a stern arch will not only look strange but will be a difficult engineering feat that ruins the lines of the boat. Better to find a boat that has some flat coachroof space or can take a stern arch without looking stupid.

So these are some things to look for when you are on YachtWorld or searching the docks. Remember that on YachtWorld there is an icon you can click labeled "Full Specs," and this will detail the equipment on board. In some cases there will be a recent survey available. For any surveys made during any future inspection of a boat, you should have a printout of either the equipment list or the survey in your hands so you can check off each item as being on board. Test what you can at the dock, but the rest will be checked at the sea trial, which is discussed next.

The Art of the Deal

"I want to go on adventures I think—not get stuck in one place. How about you?"

—Suzy in *Moonrise Kingdom*

Unless you are looking at extremely cheap boats or boats that need a lot of attention (sometimes these are one and the same), there is a good probability that you will find the cruiser of your dreams at a yacht brokerage. If you are reading this book, then by definition you are on a tight budget. So it would be in your interest to know as much as possible about the person who may hold the key to whether or not you are able to close the deal. That person is the yacht broker.

Yacht Brokers

Yacht brokers come in all flavors. In forty-eight states the business is unregulated—you pay for your business license and hang out your shingle. California and Florida have a licensing system, but there can still be issues. I recall in Dana Point, California, a case where a broker disappeared with escrow funds totaling over two million dollars.

Two of my own boats I built myself, but otherwise I have bought my cruisers via yacht brokers. In addition to these, I have also bought a few boats on behalf of clients in Florida and Taiwan. Between those purchases and working as a surveyor, I have identified quite a few distinct species of yacht brokers, and it might be helpful to review them here. Forgive me if the terminology is a little male oriented, but it is an industry dominated by males.

Mr. Down the Middle. The exact numbers of this species is hard to determine. There are many brokers who will quickly identify themselves as members of this altruistic group, claiming that they "want to treat both parties in any sale with equal fairness." But how does one really know? They may tell you something like "Don't bother with a counteroffer because it ain't gonna happen." But for all you know, the seller is on the verge of losing his house and would be willing to consider almost anything. So although I guess there are still a few of this rare breed out there, I am dubious as to how many.

The Hobbyist. These are brokers who don't really need the job or the money. This doesn't mean they don't like the job, and they may well be good at it, but they are probably retired from another job and have a decent pension coming in. They love boats, don't have to keep regular office hours, and enjoy the excuse to get away from the ball and chain once in a while. As you might suspect, they are not always very knowledgeable about boats. One time I had listed a boat of mine with a hobbyist broker, and he kept mistaking the topsides of my boat as the deck, no matter how many times I tried to convince him otherwise. "Jim," he told me by phone, "I don't see any new paint job on the topsides of your boat—just on the hull."

The Inside Tipster. This species cannot keep a secret, or so they would like you to believe. In your very first minutes of speaking with them, they start entrusting you with intimate details about the seller. "She got the boat after her husband died, so the asking price is pretty soft. He was eighty and she's about forty. My commission is doubled if I can find a buyer and her next husband at the same time. Wanna see her picture?"

The High-Ender. This species is a specialist in yachts starting at half a million dollars. They can't be bothered with small commission sales. They are easily identi-

fied because they all wear Topsiders and Guy Harvey shirts. They are concentrated in places like Newport Beach, Miami, and Fort Lauderdale. If you are reading this book, you couldn't afford to pay the taxes on his taxes, so you don't have to worry about encountering this breed.

As an experienced buyer, I suppose my favorite broker species is the hobbyist. They tend to understand that I know what I am after, so they will step back and just go through the motions. But sometimes the inside tipster can be pretty handy if you can separate the wheat from the chaff. No matter who you come across, here are some critical steps to remember to give yourself the best chance to buy at the lowest possible price.

Understand the Yacht Buying Process

Ignorance is not bliss when it comes to buying via a broker. To be fair to the broker, the seller, and yourself, you need to know how things are set up. Here are the details on how the process works, or should work.

Avoid too many fingers in the pie. Since you want to get the best price possible, make sure you are not unnecessarily involving any middlemen who could ask the selling broker for a referral fee or even a split commission. Once you find the boat on YachtWorld or whatever source, make sure you are about to phone the actual listing brokerage and not some other website or clearinghouse that is taking information from various yachts for sale and then pretending they control the boat in any way. This is surprisingly common, and in many cases is beyond the control of the legitimate listing broker.

With YachtWorld, the listing brokerage is clearly shown. You should then go to the individual brokerage website (linked directly via YachtWorld) and see if there is further information about the name of the listing broker since many brokerages have three or more brokers/salespeople within that office. Although it is rare, sometimes there will even be interoffice spiffs and tips for a broker just acting as the first point of contact by taking a phone call on behalf of the actual listing broker for a particular yacht!

This means that when you make your first phone call, your first question should be to find out the name of the broker who has the listing for the 40-foot dream boat that has caught your eye. If you have found the source, then the name of the listing broker should be forthcoming or you should be transferred right away. It is also standard practice to give out cell phone numbers of brokers since they are often out of the office, so don't be afraid to ask. If it sounds like you have reached a receptionist who has been forthcoming about the identity of the listing broker but he or she is away from the office, you can leave your contact info, but I always ask for the listing broker's cell phone number.

If you have phoned but the person answering says something like "Oh, I have to check into who has that listing. Just give me your contact info and I'll get back to you," be very wary. I prefer not to leave my contact info. Instead I continue my investigations to make sure that I am dealing with the actual broker and not a third party website that is trying to get involved with the deal to get at least a referral fee. Again, if you are on YachtWorld, that will not be an issue. The problem is with other parasitic sites that cull the data from major brokerage sites and then post them on their own.

So why do you care about a referral fee, or split commissions, or avoiding a "buyer's agent" to help you shop? Because most of these brokers are walking calculators, and on any offer you might make he will instantly distill everything down to his "net net." In other words, what will he or she pocket as a commission after he pays his buddy at the other brokerage who referred you, or the website that gave you the contact info needed to first reach you? If that commission figure is too low, he will be inclined to get you to offer closer to the full asking price in order to get his commission number up to a more acceptable figure. He may try to talk you out of submitting a low offer even if his listing agreement with his client requires him to submit one, so it is important to cut out all the possible middlemen.

So you have found a boat you are interested in, located the listing broker, and set up an appointment to see his listing. Hopefully you have not been gushing too much about how this is the boat of your dreams and you can't wait to buy it. If you have, your negotiating position has been weakened. It is fine, however, to tell the broker that you have cash or financing lined up, that you know what you want, and are not just kicking fenders.

Inspecting a Bluewater Boat

First inspections are also not the place to let your emotions run too wild. As Don Casey puts it in his book *Inspecting the Aging Sailboat:*

"When you find the very craft you have been dreaming about sulking impatiently

on a cradle or shifting restlessly in a slip,
perfect days on the water suddenly play
through your mind. You step aboard and
run your fingers over her in a lover's ca-
ress. Look how perfect she is. This is the
one! You stand at the helm, gripping the
wheel, feeling the wind through your hair,
the sun on your back, the motion of . . .
SNAP OUT OF IT!"

Obviously you need to dig deep to find out what defects are present, but generally the first things to focus on are the layout and ergonomics of the boat. Only if she passes that basic test is it even worth getting into the bilges or the engine compartment. Here is what I usually scan and analyze in the first few minutes aboard.

Is the cockpit big enough for myself and my cruising partner, or, if I am single-handing, is it set up for easy sail handling? Can I see myself and my crew sitting in this cockpit for hours or days at a time at anchor? Will there be shade enough for the two of us? Subtle things like the angle of the coamings can have a big effect on one's lower back and are not easy to change. Sit down in the cockpit at various positions to check things out.

Down below, do you have adequate headroom, especially in the galley? If you are looking at a boat in cool weather, make sure you force yourself to think hard about ventilation in the tropics, where you are doubtless headed. Hatches are difficult to retrofit, so open all the existing hatches to see what the ventilation might be like.

Are the berths big enough for me? Is that big queen "island" berth really a good sea berth on passages? Is the head really big enough for those close-quarter maneuvers? It is better to have one nice-sized head compartment instead of two Houdini-appropriate versions.

If she passes the basic layout and ergonomics tests, you can move on to a closer inspection. Now it is time to get on your knees and pull those bilge boards. Is there standing water in the bilge? A lot or a little? Pull up on the automatic switch and see if the bilge pump has been working. What about engine access? Is it so difficult that you will always be putting off necessary maintenance? Does the boat look like it has seen basic maintenance?

Are the cushions showing mold or mildew? Can you live with their color and condition? If not, it is thousands of dollars to get all interior cushions reupholstered. Is there a teak floor? If it is veneer, how is it holding up? Again, this is not the survey stage. But before you take the step of paying for the surveyor, do what you can on your own.

On deck the thing I look at first is the gelcoat. I can fix anything on a boat, including cracked and crazing gelcoat, but it is a big, messy, and detailed job that I generally avoid. And if the gelcoat is starting to go on some of the deck or the cabin sides, then chances are it is on its way to complete failure. As a rule, the gelcoat in radiused areas or with high UV exposure will go first, with the flatter or more shaded areas following later. Of course you can fill, fair, and paint over any gelcoated surface, but that is also a lot of work, so make sure you know what you are getting into. Topsides, as mentioned, are much easier to paint if the gelcoat is history.

Check the steering even if you are not yet doing a sea trial. I have seen a surprising number of deals get all the way to the sea trial stage, but once the buyer is at the helm, he or she just cannot get comfortable with the feel of the wheel or the lack of feedback in a hydraulic system. Even at a dock you can see if the steering is sloppy or stiff (possibly correctable) or just too unfamiliar. Turn the wheel lock to lock several times, fast. Can you take a comfortable stance with those big feet of yours? People were actually smaller forty years ago when your boat was designed!

If you have a cruising partner and he or she is with you, now is the time to see what might be a deal breaker. Headroom below might be okay for one crew member but not the other. If only one of you will really be in the galley, is it user-friendly for that individual? You don't want to sail thousands of miles hearing about how the galley sinks are too shallow and you know they can't be changed.

Bear in mind that if you are buying a bargain boat, there is a reason it is priced cheaply. It is certainly not going to be perfect, but there is no reason for ticking off the broker by talking down the boat at every opportunity. Find a happy medium. If it has potential, you can say so, but you also do not have to go running back to your car for your checkbook. Most brokers have dealt with dozens if not hundreds of buyers, and while it is important that you are not too effusive about what you are seeing, you also don't need to be too negative either. I always try to mention that I am appreciative that the broker is taking the time to show me a low-dollar listing.

Some boats, especially in the mild climate of coastal California, are actually in great condition despite being almost 40 years old. The original gelcoat is fine, the sails are still crisp, and the "problem" is really just lack of use by the owner. I have surveyed old Cals, Ericsons, Islanders, and Newports that looked like they had been placed in a time capsule in the early 1970s. They may have outdated electronics, but as long as a boat has a functional diesel, it can represent the best bargain. A typical story is a Marina del Rey boatowner in his seventies who bought his boat in the 1970s, used it only four times a year, and is tired of paying the escalating slip fees.

Making the Offer

Making the offer is now the big decision, but not as much of a cliff as you may think. The reason is that the buying process is really weighted in favor of you, the buyer. You will be getting a contract that, in all states, allows you several chances to escape from the deal for even the smallest of reasons. If you are using financing, then the offer can be contingent upon financing. If the financing goes through but you are not happy with a finding on the survey, you can back out or adjust the price at that point. The same applies for the sea trial.

So if your initial inspection is positive and you want to proceed, it is important to remember that you will get several bites of the apple as far as the final selling price. If you want to make a lowball offer from the very beginning, you can, but sometimes that creates a bad atmosphere and, if the offer is accepted, the broker will often stipulate that at that price the boat is sold "as is where is" and no further reductions will be considered. Since a good surveyor will always find issues with an older boat, you may want to offer something low but not completely insulting, with the knowledge that you will get further opportunities to fine-tune the price.

A deposit check is now in order, which will be handed over by you to the broker at the time he writes up the offer. The appropriate practice is for the broker to have your deposit check in hand when he phones the seller to make the offer, but that does not always happen. It is at this point, if you have cash, that you have perhaps the most leverage in this process. You should be very clear that you have cash, and also put a time limit of say 48 hours on your offer.

If you are an experienced boater and also know how the boat sails from past experience, or have already had a good look at the boat and been able to start the engine (some brokers will allow the engine to be tested upon your initial inspection), you can even make your offer "where is as is," meaning with the sea trial and survey waived. This along with your cash makes for a big incentive for the seller to accept since he knows he will have the money in his account as soon as the next day. *But this sort of offer should be made only if you were able to perform your own survey and know the design you are about to buy.* If the boat is in the water, and after you buy it you discover there are blisters all over the bottom, the problem is yours.

Surveys and Sea Trials

The sea trial and professional survey are what typically follow, assuming the seller has accepted your offer. The broker will have some surveyor names for you, but it would be best if you already have your surveyor chosen and even on notice, to avoid having the broker make his "this guy is going to call you" alert. If this happens, the surveyor may feel obligated for the referral and perhaps not be as much in your corner as you might like. So if the broker has a list of two or three names, no problem, but make the phone calls and choose the surveyor on your own. It may sound petty, but if you want an advocate for you, handle it this way.

Remember to do your best to get someone who has already surveyed the model you are looking at. Do some searching about the model on the Internet, especially on any owners association forums. If you know the name and hull number of the boat, you may even be able to learn some of its history before closing the deal. And one last tip: If you are especially impressed with the insights or online articles by a boatowner writing for an association website, and if that person is geographically close, consider inviting him to see the boat. If you can't find an adequate surveyor, you could possibly use him as a substitute for the price of a good lunch. Just be aware that the selling broker would not consider this a formal survey, and you would essentially be waiving the survey. More importantly, you would not be provided with a formal list of "items requiring correction" that a proper marine survey will turn up. This lack of detail could cost you leverage in your negotiations.

The survey is often scheduled for the same day as the sea trial. Typically, but not always, the sea trial takes place just before the survey begins. If possible, have the surveyor attend the sea trial so he can start checking systems for you and power up all electronics. One important point is to insist that the engine not be started or "warmed up" prior to your arrival. Tell the broker or his sea trial captain that you will start the trip by putting your hand on the engine block and checking that it is cold. Once you do start it up, check the diesel's exhaust for smoking and the color of any smoke. Nigel Calder in his books (see References and Further Reading) has some great detailed info on smoke color interpretation, but in general a little white smoke that clears up as the engine warms up is okay; persistent blue or black smoke is not. Zero smoke is better but rare on an older boat. Is the engine temperature stable? Even if there is wind and you are going to sail, make sure the engine gets at least 20 minutes of operation, and check it for leaks once you are back dockside.

This is no time to be shy or worry about hurting feelings. It is your money that is being put at risk, so once the boat is under way, insist on trying anything that can be turned on or off. Turn on any autopilot and use it for the entire sea trial other than some test-steering of your own. If it has a radar, find a target and check the display head for resolution and display quality. Operate all heads and pumps. You will probably be out less than an hour, so don't just sit there dreaming of Margaritaville. Take notes and keep mov-

ing. If your surveyor is on board, don't bombard him with questions that can be answered back at the dock. Concentrate on the systems, and if you have doubts you can then speak up. Is the action on that primary winch gummy, and can it be easily fixed? Does the electric windlass power up? Is the dinghy motor included, and when was the last time it ran? Does the autopilot track a course properly?

Once the sea trial is over, the survey begins in earnest. Again, it may not start the same day as the sea trial, but it often does. In some cases the boat is taken directly to a boatyard for hauling. This is typical and recommended in order to check for blisters or bottom paint issues. In particular you want to check for spalling, when there is wholesale adhesion failure of the bottom paint. If large flakes of paint are coming off, then the bottom has

STORMSAILS AND INNER FORESTAYS

With proper planning, your chances of getting caught in a serious storm are low, but as a general rule an offshore boat should be able to sail at least on a beam reach in wind of 50 knots. In these conditions, sail shape and strength are important, whereas downwind sail shape means very little.

For instance, one common tactic for sloops with roller furling jibs is to just roll out maybe 20 percent of the sail and then sheet it tight amidships, loafing downwind. If you have the sea room, this is a marginally acceptable tactic. Just make sure your roller furling line is cleated tightly, or you may have a disaster on your hands.

A few dedicated stormsails are a better idea. The sole exception might be a cutter like the Tayana 37 or the Hans Christian included here since these boats can sail with decent

performance in gale force winds with just a staysail and a triple-reefed main.

So what to have on board? First, stormsails are pretty easy to find on the used or swap meet market since they are often seen as unneeded inventory by boats up for sale after returning from a cruise (or preparing for a cruise that never happened). These sails are typically crispy new, and the only issue will be whether they are luff foil and can be loaded on your existing furler, or contain hanks for a conventional stay. If you find a good staysail candidate, the sail should be roughly 50 percent of your foretriangle if you are cruising the tropics, and 9 ounces or 10 ounces in cloth weight.

It is pretty rare these days to see a dedicated storm mainsail (called a trysail) on board even bluewater cruisers. More typical is a third reef in the *(continued next page)*

STORMSAILS AND INNER FORESTAYS, *CONTINUED*

main, or a decision already made that a staysail alone will be the final sail plan. And if you have one of those rare boats with a trysail, the odds are that it will be deployed only if you have a dedicated second sail track on the mast. This allows it to be set without unbending the mainsail.

Trysails make sense only if you practice rigging them in calm conditions with the idea of really using them when the stink hits the fan. Otherwise you may as well use the money intended for a trysail for something else (e.g., having a third reef line put into your main), especially if you have a sloop rig. Another option is to install a removable inner forestay—a fairly easy retrofit on a sloop rig. Both of my last two boats had one with a staysail already hanked on, ready to hoist.

To add this stay, there are really only a few things needed: a new bolt with tangs and a forestay hanger drilled into the mast, a good strong anchor point on deck to accept the stay, and a pair of running backstays that can either be stainless combined with a block and tackle for tensioning or just low-stretch Spectra that can also somehow be tensioned. You really do not even need a pair of staysail winches since the jib will not be flying anyway and you can use the primaries. A dedicated halyard winch would be nice, but again you can probably make use of a jib halyard winch or install a stopper.

Adding this stay moves the center of effort farther aft and also helps eliminate the risk of sailing with a partially rolled headsail in high winds. Sail shape is better, and you should expect to be able to sail with this sort of staysail in winds to 50 knots. After that, virtually all cruisers will no longer be actively sailing but either scudding off downwind (technically still sailing) or heaving-to or lying-to a sea anchor.

to be sanded or chemically peeled away until a good coat of primer or even original gelcoat is reached. Very expensive or, if you do it yourself, very tedious. The surveyor should also check underwater fittings and the prop for electrolysis. If no zincs were present at the time the boat was hauled, it is an indication that the boat was not receiving proper preventive maintenance and may have serious issues.

The findings of your surveyor are generally divided into three areas: general comments, items requiring correction for safety compliance, and recommendations by the surveyor that are not required by law but advisable. For instance, the surveyor may say that the boat is in cosmetically good condition but has some gelcoat crazing, that the batteries are not prop-

erly secured per the Code of Federal Regulations, and that the running lights are USCG compliant but poorly located on the bow and prone to immersion and failure. You can use any or all of these findings to determine whether you want to lower your offer, or you can be nonspecific and simply say that after the survey you do not wish to go forward with the deal. You are generally not obligated to provide the broker or seller with a reason, although if there is something you can point to, by all means do so. If nothing else, it will give the broker and seller a chance to offer possible solutions, sometimes via a price reduction.

The threshold question you will have to answer once you have the surveyor's findings is whether any of the findings are sufficiently serious that you either no longer want the boat or, more commonly, you want to adjust the final purchase price. An example might be that the boat was advertised with a functional radar, but it turns out that it will not power up. This may be something as simple as a fuse or as expensive as a $2,500 replacement of the entire unit. If you like the boat other than this issue, the best option is usually to leave the price as is but require that the radar be made functional during escrow and funds not be transferred until the unit is working. This approach may be rejected, however, and the seller may or may not counter with an "allowance" for the needed repair. That amount may or may not be sufficient to fix the item.

While we are on the subject of electronics, remember that many surveyors

WHAT IS A SEAWORTHY BOAT?

A fair question, and in trying to answer I was reminded of that famous reply by Supreme Court justice Potter Stewart when asked to define pornography. He answered by saying that he could not provide a precise definition, but he knew it when he saw it.

To a certain extent, my definition of a bluewater boat would also be elusive, but yes I think I know one when I see one. I won't try to put an exact number on the maximum distance between main-strength bulkheads, but the bulkhead tabbing had better be substantial and well adhered. The boat can have opening ports or hatches for ventilation, but they should be just as strong in the closed position as if there were no openings at all.

A bluewater boat is all about the fundamentals and nothing about the fluff. Radar does not make a bluewater boat, but a strong fiberglass hull from a reputable yard does. A watermaker means little, but a mast and rig that have a good chance of surviving a 360 degree roll make for a bluewater boat as well. I like side decks that have a nice gunwale to brace my foot against, but that does not mean a strong racer-cruiser cannot be considered bluewater capable as well.

My own preferences have usually trended away from the full-keel, under-canvassed, overly heavy boats that were (and sometimes still are) considered bluewater boats. How far does this go with me? Well, many pundits would not consider the Express 37 a safe offshore boat due to the fin keel, spade rudder, and light displacement. I would not hesitate to take one cruising between 30 degrees north or south. I would want an easily installed emergency rudder, but other than that there is nothing fundamentally wrong with that design in boisterous conditions. However, I know these boats to be well built. It does not mean that every fin keel spade rudder boat has the same quality.

Finally, if I have made only one point in this book, it is that a bluewater sailor can do amazing things with a boat that is anything but bluewater. Robin Lee Graham did most of his circumnavigation in a stock Cal 24. Patrick Childress circumnavigated in a beefed-up Catalina 27. And more recently Dave and Jaja Martin went around the world on a Cal 25 that Dave had rebuilt in Seattle. Much of the trip was made with two kids on board, and they capped it off with a third at the end.

My intent is not to encourage foolhardy voyages by unprepared dreamers in inadequate boats, but I will say that a bluewater sailor can do amazing things with what most pundits would deride as a design best confined to coastal waters.

do not fully test electronics and cannot really load-test batteries other than powering up, so make sure you check what you can. For example, any masthead lights are impossible to see in daylight, and you may have to ask that you be permitted to come back after dark and check. Masthead lights are very important for cruising but can be an expensive pain to fix if they are out of service.

If you cannot check lights at night, see if there is an ammeter or even a voltmeter on the electrical panel that shows a voltage drop once you flip on the masthead light. This will indicate that it is working. On the batteries, do your best to see how old they are. Most batteries are receiving a constant, life-supporting trickle charge at a slip, and if they are more than three years old cannot be counted on once you leave for cruising. They are not cheap to replace if you want quality batteries. And the seller will often assure you that the batteries are fine simply because they have never been away from shore power for more than a few hours.

The survey findings are your last and best point of leverage in the entire purchase process. On smaller boats it is possible that the surveyor will give you preliminary findings on the same day of the sea trial and survey. These will be what he sees as significant enough to warrant your attention, but it will be up to you to decide if the issues are serious enough to make any changes. The final survey will take at least 24 hours to prepare and probably longer, so it is up to you to decide on the

ENCAPSULATED VERSUS BOLT-ON KEELS

On occasion one may read of an offshore keel failure, usually on a racing boat. Any day that includes the loss of all ballast while offshore is a bad one, and can often be deadly. In the Bay Area, one of the more common boats I survey is the Santana 35, a racing sloop. This design has an extremely shallow bilge that will usually not allow an automatic bilge pump to be installed due to lack of clearance. This means that if any salt water gets into the bilge and the crew does not use the manual pump prior to running off to the yacht club bar after racing, the heads of the keel bolts will rust. In other cases the automatic bilge pumps can never get that last half inch of water out of the boat, so rust will occur. In some cases the bolts were so rusted that new "sister" bolts had to be installed next to the originals, at significant cost.

All this may point to the "encapsulated keel" as the most foolproof option for a cruising boat. This describes a boat that has been laid up with an integral keel, essentially a fiberglass shell into which ballast is then introduced. Just be aware that a bolt-on lead keel presents a significantly sleeker underwater profile that makes a big difference in performance. And, in reality, the foremen at the Taiwan boatyards I have visited admitted that lower cost is a big consideration in using encapsulated keels. Typically almost anything can be used as cheap ballast, such as lead shot, iron, steel punchings, and cement. On one fine afternoon in Kaohsiung, Taiwan, I saw a used typewriter get tossed into a keel void!

Never buy a boat with a bolt-on keel without an out-of-the-water survey. And remember that any small keel-to-hull-joint gaps may close up once the boat is hauled and placed back down on that keel, so you want your surveyor to see the boat as it is hanging in the lift, or if not possible to at least check the tightness of any nuts on the keel bolts.

purchase without having the final survey in your possession. Once you know the findings, remember that your options are:

- Do nothing and accept the boat as surveyed
- Bring up any issue(s) and ask that it be fixed before you complete the deal
- Bring up any issue(s) and explain you will accept the boat as is but at a reduced price
- Walk away from the deal entirely

If there is any final tweaking on the offer price, the broker will have to phone the seller. Sometimes this will happen while you are sitting in his office and you will know right away; otherwise, you may spend a nervous night wondering if you have your dream boat. Once you receive either an acceptance or a counteroffer or a rejection, you will know what has happened and can stop holding your breath.

A cliché becomes a cliché because it has, at its core, a basic truth. Having both bought and sold my own cruising boats about six times, I would agree that the two happiest days of a boater's life are the day he buys his boat and the day he sells it. Assuming that you have gone through with your purchase, you are on the front half of the cliché and congratulations are in order.

The List—Is Life!

Ships are the nearest things to dreams that hands have ever made.

—**Robert N. Rose**

The meat of this book is what follows: a list of twenty production cruising sailboats (plus one Honorable Mention) that are good candidates for cruising and can be purchased for under $50,000. If I had a lot of easily seized assets, I suppose this is the part where I would say "The list is not intended as a warranty that any boat chosen from the list can be safely passaged across any ocean."

Every year you can find stories of yachts abandoned at sea after the crew has activated their EPIRB locators and been plucked off still serviceable boats by rescue personnel. One should not too quickly fault these individuals for leaving a still-floating boat. After all, are they supposed to wait until it sinks beneath their feet?

The same basic instincts that draw people to the sea in mellow conditions may also draw them to dry land once they are in a crisis. According to some marine biologists, our fellow mammals—dolphins and whales—are doing much the same thing when they intentionally beach themselves when they feel a threat. But the point is that *in most cases the boat can take more than the occupants can.*

Historic Antecedent—Captain Voss' Vessel

Mind you, I am not trying to say that any boat on The List can be used for daily commutes around Cape Horn. What I am saying is that The List has yachts suitable for trade winds cruising in the tropics to take advantage of the appropriate optimum weather seasons. But if you need further convincing that the skipper is at least as important

Tilikum, an ultra-bargain cruiser with minimal electronics.

as the hull itself, it might be worth remembering that the vessel shown here nearly circumnavigated between 1901 and 1903.

The boat started its life as a dugout canoe, hollowed out from a red cedar log in the Pacific Northwest. It was already at least 50 years old when Captain John Voss bought it for $80 U.S. in gold. Voss named it *Tilikum*, decked over part of the hull, and in a series of famous passages sailed to Australia, around South Africa, and up to England. Reading from the *Venturesome Voyages of Captain Voss*, one would have to admit that truth is often stranger than fiction.

"*. . . while I was looking round about the east coast of Vancouver Island, where there are boats of all sizes and build, I came across an Indian village where I saw a fairly good-looking canoe lying on the beach. It struck me at once that if we could make our proposed voyage in an Indian canoe we would not alone make a world's record for the smallest vessel but also the only canoe that had ever circum-*navigated the globe. I at once proceeded to examine and take dimensions of the canoe, and soon satisfied myself that she was solid.*"

What's Available in the 21st Century

So while The List does not include any cedar log dugout canoes, hopefully we have made the point that boats not necessarily considered "bluewater" can make ocean passages with proper handling and preparation. Not long ago, debris from the Japanese tsunami of 2011 was washing ashore in the Pacific Northwest, to include a large fishing boat, a concrete marina dock, and multiple glass buoys. Most of it had made it across the North Pacific in about a year, averaging a knot or so in "boat" speed. If you can maintain watertight integrity in whatever craft you choose, your odds of complete disaster are pretty slim. A far greater risk, statistically, is falling overboard.

In compiling The List for this book, I certainly realized I was not breaking new ground as far as the overall concept. John Kretschmer put together a nice collection based on his great detailed reviews in *Sailing* magazine, and Gregg Nestor wrote *Twenty Affordable Sailboats to Take You Anywhere*. Kretschmer, in particular, deserves a close following due to the tremendous amount of sea miles and actual hands-on experience he has with many of the boats he reviews. Others have not written books on the subject but provide some excellent choices via websites or, in the case of John Neal, client consulting.

But aside from a bit of an East Coast bias in most of the used-boat literature, one of the things that concerned me was that for most would-be cruisers, it was their budget that was the overriding limitation. In other words, if my premise is that most people can come up with at least a $50,000 purchase budget, what are some of the possible options given that threshold? That was the starting point, and then I added the other filters based on my own biases, which I am sure some will find fault with.

Some industry pros reading The List may dismiss a few of the boats as "outdated IOR designs" (International Offshore Rule, a measurement rule for racing sailboats; see sidebar). Others, especially the armchair sailors, may whip out their calculators and say that the comfort ratio on a given boat is only—heaven forbid—29.2! Comfort ratio? Please—even Ted Brewer, who invented the formula and designs some sweet boats, says in his book *Understanding Boat Design* that it is all very relative:

"Do consider, though, that a sailing yacht heeled by a good breeze will have a much steadier motion than one bobbing up and down in light airs on left over swells from yesterday's blow; also that the typical summertime coastal cruiser will rarely encounter the wind and seas that an oceangoing yacht will meet. Nor will one human stomach keep down what another stomach will handle with relish, or with mustard and pickles for that matter! It is all relative."

There are just too many variables that can affect a boat's motion for the comfort ratio to be used as a deal breaker. Is the boat going on a trade winds circumnavigation, which will be almost all downwind? How loaded will it be beyond its original displacement? Does the skipper tend to sail the boat to its limits, or is he or she more conservative? How are the stores distributed down below? Is the anchor locker full of ⅜ chain when 5⁄16 would have been better? Is there a 300-pound dinghy and motor hanging off the stern on davits?

On yachts less than 45 feet, the distribution of stores and the location of tankage are critical if you are provisioning for months at a shot. These factors can have a great effect on the boat's motion through the water. Other factors are the boat's fuel capacity and/or the willingness of the skipper to use the motor instead of wallowing in a cross swell with not enough wind to sail. In my case I like a boat with enough tankage to motor up to 25 percent of my longest passage at 4 knots. Even this low speed can make a big difference in keeping the boat's motion comfortable if the wind is too light to sail. It also can make a huge difference to crew morale and comfort by keeping some air flowing through the boat. So the comfort ratio index often takes a distant second to various other factors.

I also believe that there is often a bit

RATINGS RULES AND THEIR EFFECT ON RACER-CRUISERS

The International Offshore Rule (IOR) was a popular racing handicap measurements system, especially in the 1970s. But, as Wikipedia notes, there were some design issues that compromised seaworthiness. "The IOR rule encouraged wide short boats with limited stability. A narrow waterline and large beam on deck, combined with a high center of gravity, meant that crew weight provided a significant proportion of stability at small heel angles, and boats had a relatively low angle off vanishing stability." Narrow waterlines and large beams also do not make for downwind tracking ability. A quick scan of the designs included here may lead some to scoff that The List is primarily a bunch of old IOR racer-cruisers available at low prices.

In reality only the C & C 40 and the Pearson 40 have an IOR heritage. The Newport 41, for instance, was designed to the old Cruising Club of America (CCA) racing rules, which did not provoke the extreme and sometimes unwieldy waterline design tweaking that the IOR did. This does not mean that the Newport 41 or the C & C 40 track downwind "as if on rails" (a common desire amongst cruisers). They can be a challenge to steer downwind in big seas, especially if too much mainsail is up and the boat is being pushed rather than pulled. But they are not as squirrelly to handle as some IOR racer-cruisers. And, in the case of the Pearson 40, an aftermarket rudder improvement did in fact improve downwind tracking ability.

too much overanalysis and sheer snobbery when it comes to the discussions on cruising boats. This is one of the reasons why my reviews do not go into the level of detail that other reviewers may prefer. I have seen in various online forums some incredible, almost slavish deference to any negative comment in a design review. Something like "Well I was going to make an offer on one of those South Seas 40s, but the review in *Practical Sailor* said that the cockpit was probably too large for any boarding seas."

Really? Okay, but didn't you say that the specific boat you found was in good condition, had a rebuilt diesel, was loaded with electronics, and had a new inflatable? Maybe you could simply set a life raft canister into the footwell of that cockpit and help reduce the volume. Or increase the size of the drains. Or take into consideration that many boats have circumnavigated without taking a wave in the cockpit.

These reviews are intended to provide some candidates for cruising based on my own direct experience and, yes, biases. Some folks will scoff, laugh, or demur. Others may rethink whether they really need to spend $250,000 on a gold-plater and, by getting something more affordable, go next year instead of in a decade. If Venturesome Voss could do it in his cedar log canoe, perhaps you don't need your boat to be perfect either. This does not mean that you should buy the next sailboat you find within your budget and take off. It means just that there is not always the perfect boat, the perfect crew, or the perfect plan.

The List is intended to whet the appetite and stimulate further investigation of a specific design. I do not feel it is necessary to analyze the placement of every cleat or the lack of a dedicated shower stall. I remember one cruiser who sincerely preferred that the factory had combined the shower function into the head compartment because it meant he could wash everything down at the same time that he was bathing!

What may be a deal breaker to some might not be to another. My focus is on reasonable performance under sail and power, a usable interior plan, overall value, and reasonable build quality. Where possible I tried to contact the actual designer of the boat, if alive, and in all cases was at least able to get input from knowledgeable owners.

Criterion for Inclusion in The List

A lot of excellent boats that are available for under the 50K threshold do not appear here, including some of my favorites. As for my parameters for a design to make it onto The List, what follows are some of the key qualifiers.

Number of Hulls Produced

There is not much point in writing about designs that had a very limited production run and will be almost impossible for a reader to locate. The general cutoff I used was a hundred hulls, which sometimes included several redesigns dubbed Mark 2, Mark 3, and so forth. Assuming that at least a hundred of any given design were still in North America, and at any given time maybe 20 percent were for sale, there should be at least a few available to look at on either coast. I did let the CSY slip in as a qualifier with only ninety made, but the Pearson 40 was relegated to "Honorable Mention" status since only seventy-one were produced.

Minimum Length of 35 Feet

Yes, you can circumnavigate in a 26-footer, but given that used boats are now in-

credibly accessible, why not consider a reasonable size that can carry the stores you need, provide a comfortable ride, and achieve a reasonable hull speed? There is a big difference in interior accommodation, stability, and stowage capacity in a 35-footer as compared to a 30-footer. But a 35-footer is still manageable as it can use 5/16 chain, a 25 pound anchor, sails with luff lengths no more than 40 feet, etc.

Factory Built

Kit boats finished by an owner-builder were not considered for The List because the quality varies too much. There are a lot of Westsails out there (a few were factory finished) and a lot of Bruce Roberts designs, but to have practical value I focus on production vessels. I will say that some of the nicest boats I have ever seen were owner built, but unfortunately there is just no way to quantify or qualify them for the purposes of a book like this. If you are so inclined, my short list of owner-built boats that I would consider looking into would include the Corbin 39 and the Cape George 38.

Reasonable Performance (Sail)

This is my personal bias, but The List does not have many crab crushers that could not sail off a lee shore without the diesel redlined. For safety we also prefer a Capsize Screening Number under 2.0, which is a subjective but still useful threshold for offshore safety. The selections are not undercanvassed, as is often the case, and are meant to be sailed in any decent breeze.

I have met many circumnavigators in the course of my work in the tropics, mostly as they were finishing their circuit as they came north from Panama. A large number of these boats were heavy Taiwan Teakies that had to fire up the diesel if the wind dropped below 12 knots. The owners had in many cases doubled the fuel tankage on their boats, and many of those I talked to said they would opt for more performance if there was a next time.

Reasonable Performance (Power)

Cruisers spend a lot of time motoring. In the designs chosen, the typical engine installed at the factory was a diesel and was big enough to push the boat through the conditions often seen while cruising. When selecting my own boats, I have also made engine access a priority, and it is often discussed here but not in any objective way. Perhaps this is because at six foot two and north of two hundred pounds, what I consider "inaccessible" may be fine for a smaller skipper.

INSIDE THE NUMBERS

There are also several numbers shown on the individual design specifications that warrant a little explanation. The first is the ominously named Capsize Screening Number—an action that you would obviously prefer to avoid with your boat. (See below for how these numbers are derived.) Next is the Sail Area to Displacement (SA/D) Ratio, and finally the Displacement to Length (D/L) (at waterline) Ratio. Just remember that trying to reduce all the variables that go into a capsize into a finite number is of only limited value.

The SA/D Ratio is a static and immutable number in what is an inherently dynamic environment—the open ocean. There are many other factors that are at least as important in keeping a boat safe in Force 8 conditions—dynamic stability, weight distribution, the experience level of the helmsman, etc.

Perhaps the best illustration of dynamic stability can be seen on my favorite YouTube video, a helicopter shot of Larry Ellison's ultralight racer *Sayonara* in the infamous 1998 Sydney-Hobart race. Just Google the three words "sailing big waves" and the one-minute video should come up at the top of your screen.

In the video, *Sayonara* is leading the race on a screaming beam reach halfway across the Bass Strait, her blade jib sheeted in tight and her reefed main eased off due to gusts over 60 knots. The swells are running at 30 feet, and at one point the boat flies off the face of a wave at 15 knots and then shudders visibly as she smacks down on landing.

On the video, watch her angle of heel carefully. It does not vary more than a few degrees through the entire sequence due to the tremendous dynamic stability she is generating with her sail trim, forward speed, and efficient fin keel and spade rudder. It's the same principle as riding your bike slowly and trying to take your hands off the handlebars—pretty hard at slow speed but easier if the bike is going faster and has more dynamic stability.

Sayonara went on to win that race, in which 115 boats started but only 44 finished. Six sailors died as winds peaked at 70 knots. So while it may be tempting to conclude that you are always better off weathering a gale offshore in a Westsail 32 than an Express 37, I personally would not jump to that conclusion. The Express 37, for instance (a popular Northern California racing design), is a boat that can scud off before large waves at a nice speed and still maintain excellent control, whereas the Westsail would perhaps be a better candidate for heaving-to or even lying ahull.

Different designs may call for different tactics, but various approaches can be successful. As mentioned, there are numerous examples of boats being *(continued next page)*

INSIDE THE NUMBERS, *CONTINUED*

abandoned in a blow, only to find the boat floating safely and drifting downwind months later. With Search and Rescue (SAR) communications and response so highly developed, it is often proven that the boats can take more in an offshore blow than the crew can.

$$\text{Capsize Number} = \text{Beam}/(\text{Displacement}/64)^{1/3}$$

All other factors being equal (such as payload distribution, amount of sail actually up, etc.), a boat with a lower capsize number is stiffer and inherently more stable than one with a higher number. In general, a number less than 2 is considered acceptable for an "offshore" design. Obviously this calculation is not used for multihulls such as the Prout 37, which is a conservative multihull design with tremendous initial stability.

$$\text{Sail Area to Displacement Ratio} = \text{Sail Area}/(\text{Displacement}/64)^{2/3}$$

In simplest terms, this ratio indicates the speed potential of a boat in light wind. The higher the number, the faster the boat, at least in light air and probably in all wind speeds.

Cruising sailboats have ratios between 10 and 15.

Performance cruisers have ratios between 16 and 20.

Racing sailboats have ratios above 20.

High-performance racers have ratios above 24.

$$\text{Displacement to Length (D/L) Ratio} = \text{Displacement in Long Tons} \div (0.01 \times \text{LWL})^3$$

A boat with a higher displacement for a given length is inherently heavier and therefore slower, though it would be erroneous to conclude that a heavier boat is always stronger or more seaworthy. A boat with a D/L above 325 is considered a cruiser; below 200 a racer; and between 200 and 325 a compromise or racer-cruiser.

No More than 30 Years Old

Once a boat goes over 25 years old, if the wiring and plumbing are original, you are asking for problems. In some cases the diesel may be fine, and even the hull, but are you sure the rigging is not also original? Even a surveyor may not be able to tell. Note that I am not ruling out boats designed in the 1970s, but to make The List the design would have to have been built into at least the 1980s. In addition, many marinas and insurance companies have an age limit that precludes accepting boats that are over 30 years old, which will affect access and resale once your cruising days are over. The oldest boat included here is probably the Pearson 40, which was made only until 1981 and is therefore just over the limit.

Hands-on Experience

With a few exceptions, I have either sailed, surveyed, or inspected all these designs. Since I have been based primarily on the West Coast, there will be a bias that way. But most of these boats are small enough that they could be trucked cross-country, and models have been sold on both coasts. Just as you will find more older Ericsons on the West Coast, you will also find more Freedoms on the East Coast.

Available for Under $50,000 USD

I have seen examples of all these designs sold for under $50,000. Some are substantially lower, and some will be right at that number but will ultimately sell for less. That cutoff is pretty simple, at least to my way of thinking, because if someone wants to go cruising badly enough, he or she should be able to save $50,000 within several years.

One very practical method is to come up with a down payment and buy the boat financed, with no prepayment penalty, and then move on board. This should immediately save you money and allow you to ease into the cruising lifestyle and fine-tune the boat. After all if you can't cope with living on a boat at a dock with your car and grocery stores near, how will you do "out there?"

Take a second job, sell that second car, downsize your apartment, or if you are lucky simply sell your condo. Pretty much any warm body can get $50,000 together. If you can't, then you simply don't want it badly enough.

So there you have it. But I really want to close these chapters by repeating the most fundamental lesson I have learned about cruising. The amount of fun you will have is not directly proportional to the length of your boat or the balance of your bank account. If you buy a budget cruiser and anchor next to a fully tricked out 50-footer, your potential score on the Fun Meter will be just as high. You can still snorkel the same reefs, see what your son's face looks like without being engrossed in a video game, and explore the world while carrying your plastic turtle shell with you.

Most of the boats that follow are not candidates for high-latitude sailing, but don't most of us dream more about sailing into quiet lagoons, having a potluck on the beach with fellow cruisers, and no longer worrying about gridlock on the interstate? If you have a desire to cross the Magellan Strait and commune with the penguins, take a look at a Ted Brewer pilothouse design built in aluminum. Otherwise, read onward.

Without further qualifications (drum roll please), I give you—The List . . . .

The Niagara 35 is the shortest boat on The List but still offers an impressive mix of classic looks and a modern underbody from a respected builder. This is Trident, a 1987 version shown sailing in the Round Howe Island Race in Canada. Note the salty little bow pulpit, which moves the anchor roller forward and clear of the hull. (Courtesy owner John Williamson)

Niagara 35

There is an undeniable, head-turning saltiness to the Niagara 35. Maybe it's the little bowsprit, which usually has at least one anchor hanging off it, or the traditional boxy trunk cabin. Cruising sailors tend to be fairly conservative, and this boat lives up to their expectation of what a cruising sailboat should look like.

To a certain extent, it seems there is only so much that can be done with the interior of monohull cruising sailboats less than 40 feet. The majority will have a quarter berth plus the galley aft, a settee across from a dinette, and then forward a head plus the ubiquitous V-berth (which tends to be used as a garage for boats on offshore passages).

The original version of this boat was one that prospective buyers seemed to either love or hate. With the first "Classic" version of the Niagara 35, designer Ellis tried to turn the typical interior around completely. To the armchair sailor reviewing a layout drawing on a piece of paper, the design seems logical. The interior is divided into two distinct sections, with berths both port and starboard upon descending the companionway. Upon opening a door to port, you enter the galley and main cabin, which may have had some advantages in a seaway (with less room to be sent flying as the boat heaved along) but definitely made for a less open, compartmentalized interior. Since the forward V-berth is given up completely, there is an especially commodious dinette across the entire beam of the boat.

I can't speak from experience, but with the Classic it seems to me that the separating bulkhead dividing the cabins makes for great privacy but may affect ventilation. Ventilation is everything in trade winds cruising, so my instinct would be that the Classic is better suited for cooler climes, and I would opt for the later redesign if headed for the tropics. But it is hard to deny the berthing options that are offered with this unique design, and owners with kids like Michael Haldane of *Atelier* (see owner comments) are very happy with the Classic.

The later "Encore" version that came out in 1984 was more conventional and very sought after on the used market. Although I have never sailed a Niagara, I did get aboard the Encore version once in Newport Beach. I especially liked the double berth that the Encore uses forward in lieu of a V-berth, and a spacious head compartment. It took me a while to decide if I liked the bowsprit, but ultimately I decided it was useful for keeping the anchor clear of the bow and, according to the seller, did not create any undue weather helm with the headstay placement. And, yes, it is kind of salty.

Early models of the Niagara 35 had saildrives installed—not rare today but highly unusual for its time. As long as electrolysis was kept in check, these units

Years Produced	1978–1990
Designer	Mark Ellis
Estimated Hulls Produced	290
Length Overall	35 feet
Length at Waterline	26 feet 6 inches
Draft	5 feet 6 inches
Beam	11 feet 5 inches
Sail Area	598 square feet
Capsize Number	1.9
SA/D	16.5
D/L	335
Displacement	14,000 lbs.
Ballast	7,100 lbs.
Typical Engine	Westerbeke/Universal 27 hp
Fuel Capacity	30 gallons
Water Capacity	80 gallons
Typical Price Range	$25,000–$50,000 USD (Encore model in higher range)
Most Active Owners Association	http://ca.groups.yahoo.com/group/ niagara35sailboatowners/

Hinterhoeller Yachts

Niagara 35 Encore

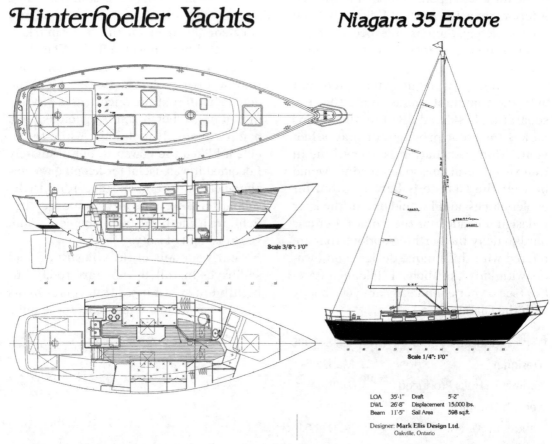

Scale 3/8": 1'0"

Scale 1/4": 1'0"

LOA	35'-1"	Draft	5'-2"
DWL	26'-8"	Displacement	15,000 lbs.
Beam	11'-5"	Sail Area	598 sq.ft.

Designer: **Mark Ellis Design Ltd.**
Oakville, Ontario

The Niagara 35 Classic was superseded by the Encore which has a more conventional open interior. The Encore version generally commands at least 10 percent more on the resale market, partly due to its being a few years newer and also because it proved to have the more popular layout. (Courtesy Niagara Owners Association)

were reliable and efficient with the prop wash thrown directly back instead of partially downward as with standard shafts. Later models had V drives, which do not deliver full output to the prop. But since they were usually coupled to a bigger Westerbeke, most owners I contacted were happy with the power provided.

All the Niagaras had spade rudders standard, and I could not find complaints about them in my research. But there is no denying that spade rudders are slightly

more exposed than those that are attached to skegs or keels, and there will be some purists who will keep looking just because of this. If this is the size boat you want, I am not sure I would pass up a Niagara that was in good condition, well equipped, and attractively priced just because it did not use a skeg rudder. But that's just me.

A fair number of these Canadian Niagaras have never seen salt water, so it is possible to find a 30-year-old Niagara 35 that looks like it is not long out of the factory. It is truly amazing to see what the difference can be between a boat that has never seen salt water (or excessive sunlight) and one that has been in salt water its entire life.

Since many of these boats are on the Great Lakes, an East Coast sailor could make a vacation out of passaging on his new purchase via the Erie Canal out to New York. A West Coast sailor could hopefully find one in the Pacific Northwest, or if the price was right could justify what would probably be around $5,000 to truck it from the Great Lakes westward.

The Good, the Bad, and the Ugly

The original interior layout is unique in a boat this size. If you make long passages and find the V-berth useless for sleeping at sea, the aft berths in this configuration may appeal to you, especially if you have kids or are using pickup crew. Nice raised gunwales along the deck make for safer footing offshore. There is also a strong and devoted owners association that can help

out with the inevitable issues that arise with an older boat.

On the negative side, the flat coach-roof sides and relatively large windows are not as resistant to a large boarding beam sea, though I would not call it a deal breaker. The installation of a dodger is a bit awkward as well. And of course this is a balsa-cored design; you will want to make sure yours is sound at the time of purchase and stays that way. The boat also has a short waterline and therefore lower theoretical hull speed, lower than any other boat included here.

I have owned a saildrive boat and am not as afraid of them as some. But it is true that you have aluminum constantly in salt water and subject to electrolysis, with maintenance being a bit more difficult than a straight-shaft drive. Remember that only earlier models sported the small saildrive, however, so this may not even come up as an issue in your search.

Ugly? Not hardly. Mark Ellis always seems to include a nice sheer and bal-

As with many Canadian boats, dark topside colors were a popular option for the Niagara 35. However, for cruising in the tropics, white or off-white can make for a slightly cooler interior. (Courtesy Jim Eastland)

anced proportions in his work. I would rate this boat and the Morgan 382 as the best incarnations of a visually appealing small cruiser. These boats have a strong following for a reason.

Owner Comments

"My wife and I have two boys aged 9 and 12. The "Classic" interior is amazing for its versatility and flexible privacy options. So far it has been a fantastic family-friendly design. It adapts to changing needs and it's nice to be able to have options simply by closing doors etc. She has the original Westerbeke W40 diesel with a Paragon V drive. I have really enjoyed this mechanical setup for the endless torque and reliability of design."

—Michael Haldane, owner of *Atelier*

Below are a number of features of the boat that John William, owner of *Trident*, has come to value:

- *Large bilge*
- *Larger engine (we motor more than we admit)*
- *Serious under-deck access to all deck hardware and great access to tankage with large access plates—you can get at stuff you need to repair*
- *Simple rig that can be singlehanded and good in heavy air (with the addition of a boom vang). Artful use of a double-block mainsheet system enables you to fine-tune the mainsail for light air sailing/racing*
- *Strong lead keel with flat base for stable cradle and resting on the hard capability*
- *Secure yet spacious cockpit decent for entertaining and excellent for bouncy sea conditions*
- *Big foretriangle that allows you to go to windward even under jib alone*

- *Good locker space (something that many modern boats are increasingly lacking) to hide stuff. The Classic has more locker space than the Encore, but the Encore has more than most modern boats.*

What would John William improve?

Well, she points well, but moving the main shrouds inboard would give her another 5 degrees pointing.

The curved sheer and reverse transom make her look pretty, but the stern ladder is an instrument of torture. Modern boats often have fuller quarters and the blessings of a stern platform (but I think you lose on the performance and safety side unless these wide-open sterns are conservatively designed, a la Island Packet).

For offshore cruising, some would prefer a skeg on the rudder (although I have never heard of Niagara rudder failure).

"My 1978 Niagara 35 is hull #10—the traditional model, with three—more like two and a half—cabins if you count the forepeak cabin as a half. It's great for sail storage, a kids' berth, or even a small workshop as some have configured it. The best thing about the layout is the ability to sleep one couple/family in the aft cabin quarter berths and another family or couple in the main saloon—potentially with kids in the forepeak berths—while having independent access to the head. And the main cabin folks can make breakfast in the galley (quietly) while letting the quarter-berthed people sleep in.

"I have never had a problem with the saildrive. I recently replaced the rubber seal—which was over 25 years old and in pretty good shape. I had water access into the oil of the saildrive one year, but

when the seal was fixed the unit worked fine—pretty forgiving and tough. I have a big prop on the business end—16 × 12— that hasn't caused any problem."

—Dennis Draper, owner of
Margaret Dawn

"I wanted to purchase the Encore, but due to the price differential and local availability at the time of my purchase, I went with the Traditional (Classic). I have to say that after using the boat for 5 years I am very glad I bought the Traditional. Off

watch we can use the saloon in as much privacy as is possible in a 35-foot boat. This assumes that the V-berth would not be usable in offshore conditions due to motion. It has better heat retention in the saloon (stock boat not insulated) during shoulder seasons, and excellent sail stowage in the bow with good access to the foredeck. I actually do swap furling headsails."

—Barry Zadjlik, owner of hull #87,
Keyanow

We're not in Catalina anymore, Toto. Wind Star was cruised by Kiwi sailor Rob Kyles all over the South Pacific, purchased from the original owner who sailed her from North America to New Zealand. This is Isle of Pines in New Caledonia. (Courtesy Rob Kyles)

Catalina 36

I admit that, for the longest time, I had the same anti-Catalina snobbery that many forum rats seem to demonstrate. Maybe Frank Butler, the visionary Catalina founder, should have named his company Patagonia or Gale Force. But the reality is that Butler knew that the majority of his customers were never going to Cape Horn or even the South Pacific. They might, just might, head out to Catalina Island. So he built his boats with great inherent value and almost nothing spent on advertising for many decades. Word of mouth and a strong dealer network have kept Catalina as the only major sailboat manufacturer in the United States in continuous operation since 1970.

I became a bigger Catalina fan in 1989. The 42 had just come out, and I was hired to take a couple out to the Channel Islands for a three-day cruise. We left Channel Islands Harbor as the wind got up to its usual 18 knots, and the fully battened mainsail went up without a fuss. We cleared the breakwater and unrolled a new 120, which set perfectly. The helm was well balanced, and we scalloped out to Santa Cruz Island on one glorious 4-hour tack. The Catalina was, and still is, the best 42 for the money I have ever sailed.

As I started to survey the 36s a few years later, I took

another look at just what Catalina offered. After all, if Patrick Childress could take a reinforced Catalina 27 around the world, maybe the 36 could go offshore as well. Moreover, with 1,800 built of just the original version and 3,000 overall, it is hard to ignore such a popular design that has a median resale price well below the $50,000 threshold of this book.

The photo that leads the chapter is *Wind Star*, which was sailed by its original American owner to New Zealand before being purchased by Kiwi Rob Kyles, who then cruised the South Pacific. In addition to *Wind Star*, singlehander Mike Gartland took his *Alaskan Poor Boy* to New Zealand and back after he converted the boat to a cutter rig. Eileen Ross and Don Elmore sailed their 36 *Moonrise* 8,000 miles from Seattle to Europe. And the Catalina 36 *Patriot*, skippered by Craig Mortensen, finished a circumnavigation in 2009. If you look at the photos of the *Patriot* on the Catalina website, you can clearly see an early-model Catalina 36 under the custom canvas, radar tower, and windvane steering bolted to the transom.

So before the online forum rats quickly dismiss Catalinas as not being bluewater capable, they might consider these stories. The 42, in particular, is proving to be a popular cruising boat and was actually designed by the Nelson Marek design house.

When I spoke with designer Gerry Douglas in Florida, he told me that the 36 was the first Catalina that was his own design. He had been with Catalina only a

Years Produced	1982–1995 (Mark I)
Designer	Gerry Douglas
Estimated Hulls Produced	1,800
Length Overall	35 feet 6 inches
Length at Waterline	30 feet 4 inches
Draft (shoal/deep keel)	4 feet 5 inches/5 feet 10 inches
Beam	11 feet 11 inches
Sail Area	555 square feet (601 for tall rig)
Capsize Number	1.93
Sail Area/Displacement Ratio	15.8 (tall rig)
Displacement/Length Ratio	241
Displacement	15,000 lbs. average
Ballast	6,000 lbs.
Typical Engine	Universal 25 hp
Fuel Capacity	25 gallons
Water Capacity	72 gallons
Typical Price Range	$30,000–$50,000 USD
Most Active Owners Association	www.catalina36.org
Owner Blogs	http://windstar.jimdo.com/

Perhaps the most unique feature on the Catalina 36 is the big double berth tucked under the cockpit, although it is probably too stuffy for sleeping in the tropics, where the V-berth would be a better option. (Courtesy Catalina Yachts)

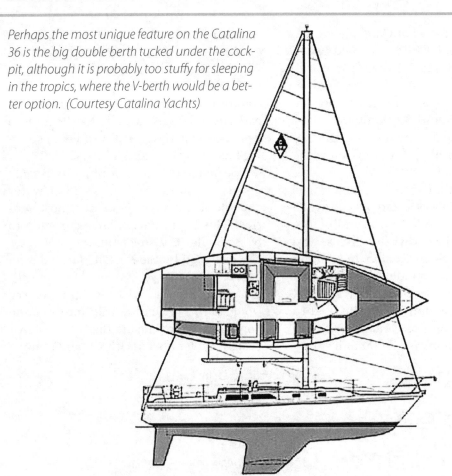

short time before owner Frank Butler (who was heavily involved in all previous boats) finally eased off the reins enough for a designer like Douglas to exercise full control. Douglas also explained that from the waterline down, the Mark II, which came out in 1994, was the same design as the earlier version, in order to continue racing with the same handicap.

"I flared it above the waterline aft, so the cockpit is larger, plus the aft bunk is easier to access. We started modifying the transom even in the later Mark I hull numbers, but the Mark IIs have the cutout transom and swim step."

Douglas also made some minor interior changes over the years, but overall the philosophy seemed to be that there was little reason to mess with the most popular 36-footer ever built. I have surveyed quite a few and would offer the following comments.

At 6 foot 2 inches, I love the fact that I still have an inch over my head when down below on this design. As with many boats this size, you step down over a ladder straddling the engine box, which when removed will almost always reveal a Universal diesel. The M25 is typical and is adequate to move this design. Access is superb, including to the stuffing box via the aft cabin.

Inside, teak was used on most vertical surfaces and shelving, but the tables (one dinette and one "card table" to starboard) are plain vanilla, using imitation wood grain Formica. Practical but of course more of an RV look than might be desired. Both tables will drop down onto chocks to convert to berthing. The chainplates carry down an impressive 4 feet from deck level and are prominently displayed where they are attached on the main bulkhead forward.

The galley is to port. If you are looking at an earlier model that still has the original alcohol stove, bear in mind that by the time you buy everything needed to switch to LPG, the investment could be close to $2,000. On the other hand, if you are looking at a boat that has everything you want except a tired original diesel, this is one of the easiest boats I have ever seen for swapping out the auxiliary. Dropping in a new Yanmar would not be difficult for anyone moderately handy, as long as the selling price reflects the investment needed, and of course as long as you know what you are getting into.

For me the head compartment in the 36 is as refreshing as the headroom. Most head compartments on boats this size range require Houdini-like gymnastics in order to take a shower. But designer Douglas allowed for ample room, and on later models added an extra door for direct access from the forepeak.

Douglas was kind enough to provide a chronology of the various refinements indexed by hull number, incorporated not necessarily by model year but essentially added to the production line as soon as they were ready.

"The first cutaway transom to create a walk-through was in 1989, #1040. This was a MKI model and the 'walk-through' *was offered briefly as an option. The first MKII was prototyped on hull #1365, and started with hull #1368 in May 1994. Although hull #1373 was a MKI, I am sure there was a good reason for this but I don't have a record of it. Whenever we changed anything, no matter how much better, there was always someone who wanted it the 'old way.' The first boat with an enclosed aft cabin was hull #1192, January 1992. Regarding blisters, we had our problems in the 1980s like all builders did. We used Glidden Blister Guard gelcoat for several years. This worked until the gelcoat was sanded through. We then went to a vinylester laminate directly behind the gelcoat, which solved the blister problem. There were very occasional blister issues after that, but these were attributed to other causes such as bottom paint preparation and were not gelcoat osmotic blisters."*

Of course the blister bugaboo can be a serious issue. As Kiwi Robby Kyles of *Wind Star* described, his early Mark I had to have the gelcoat stripped below the waterline. Not all model years were affected equally, and given that whatever boat you look at will be at least 15 years old, an out-of-the-water survey will quickly show whether your specific boat has an active osmosis issue to deal with. Boats launched after 1995 used vinylester resin, with blisters virtually eliminated.

Returning down below, the Catalina 36 was one of the first production boats to adopt a full-sized berth/cabin under the cockpit. In a seaway this area would be preferable to the forepeak, and there is just enough headroom for a crew member to shimmy out of his foulies from a sitting position. Of course this means that cockpit stowage will suffer, and the 36 has only a shallow cockpit locker on the port side plus two smaller cubbies aft by the helm.

At the time the Catalina 36 came out in 1982, it was still unusual to have all the halyards led aft for cockpit control. But it was an instant success and expanded to all Catalina models quite quickly. My sailing experiences on the 36 have all been day sails, so I can't speak to how she behaves in a 10-foot following sea, but during my sea trials the design balanced well and the mainsheet traveler was easy to trim. The rig is as simple as it gets, with single spreaders, double lowers, and a keel-stepped painted mast on the older boats. Many of the newer 36s used a Charleston Spars furling main, but most of these may edge out of the $50,000 price range we are limited to.

The Good, the Bad, and the Ugly

Good would probably start with availability. Almost 1,800 were built of just the Mark I, and since the interior layout is well known, a buyer can focus on things like electron-ics, engine, and asking price. It would even be easy to find a sister ship to check out locally before driving or flying a longer distance to see a boat actually for sale.

These boats sail well and offer a very cruisable interior. The finish level is adequate inside. The outside offers little personality but is certainly utilitarian, and the wide side decks help offset the lack of any real gunwale. Up forward, retrofitting an electric windlass on the Mark I would not be easy due to the recessed locker well.

There were so many of these boats built that surveyors have a pretty good idea what to look for as to weak spots. The forestay fitting (through-bolted into the forward part of the anchor well) has sometimes shown heavy corrosion, and like many sailboats using flush-mount windows, these have been known to leak. I would say that at least half the boats I have looked at showed some kind of attempt by the owner to stop leaks at these windows, with varying results.

Ugly would apply only if you came

Wind Star sailing with triple-reefed main in the Ha'apai island group in Tonga. The dinghy may be suspect to a large boarding sea in nastier conditions, but on a 36-footer this is still a far better configuration than hanging the dinghy from davits. (Courtesy Rob Kyles)

across a boat with unresolved blister issues. And I have to admit that I wish this boat had a bit more than just the molded-in toe rail for those going forward in a seaway. Boats like the Morgan 382 win points in this regard.

Comments from Designer
Gerry Douglas

"Although the 36 was never at the high end of the price range against the competition, and we tried to be as efficient in the building process as possible, I was never under pressure to cut corners or 'decontent' the 36 to reach a price point.

"I was always looking for ways to make the 36 a better boat for our customers, and this was rewarded by continued sales for many years and owner loyalty.

"When people shopping for a used boat ask me if there are better years than others, I can honestly tell them to buy the newest one they can afford because the 36 really did get better every year. We didn't make model year changes. The 36 was always changing, and I would incorporate changes to gear and systems as design features as they were available and ready for production. It didn't make sense to me to hold off an improvement for an arbitrary 'model year' date. The 36 was built to plans approved by ABS [American Bureau of Shipping] for Offshore Racing Yachts, and ABYC [American Boat and Yacht Council] recommendations were followed that were applicable to the 36.

"Regarding the dinette/settee on the starboard side, this was actually one of the more popular features of the 36. All boats were shipped with all the cushions required to convert the dinette to a settee or berth with the table lowered. Many of these boats were cruised by a couple who would lower the table on the port side, install the filler cushions provided, and leave it in that position as a lounging space for watching TV or reading and use the two-person dinette on the starboard side for dining. This feature has been incorporated into several other Catalina models since the 36—with good customer acceptance."

Owner Comments

"One of the main things that drew us to buy Wind Star was the warm, inviting, spacious, and well-laid-out interior. For us it was important that we felt at home considering the length of time we would spend aboard. Sailing performance and strength were very important to get to the destination safely, and to cap it off she is a good-looking boat with few impractical extremes of design.

"For our purpose [going offshore from New Zealand to the South Pacific Islands], the Catalina 36 needed a number of modifications: a removable inner forestay for stormsails; solar and wind power; an underdeck autohelm, etc. However, there are no features we really dislike that we have not been able to alter or mitigate.

"Worst aspects? The fixed portlights and the anchor well have leaked many times, but they are mostly watertight now. The gelcoat on our boat [below waterline] had considerable osmosis—more cosmetic than structural—which had to be peeled and new layers of fiberglass laid with an epoxy barrier coat."

—Robby Kyles, owner Catalina 36
　　Wind Star

Although designed by Raymond Wall forty years ago, the CS 36T is still a smart-looking sailer and one of the best-built boats available for under $50,000. This is Bob Thompson's Heron. (Courtesy Bob Thompson)

Canadian Sailcraft 36T

The Canadian Sailcraft 36 seems to have achieved a rare consensus opinion amongst many reviewers over the decades as a high-quality and sweet-sailing boat. In fact, there were so many positive reviews by authorities, including *Practical Sailor, Good Old Boat,* and John Kretschmer, that I had to seek a boat out for myself. Finally, in Brisbane Marina, south of San Francisco, I came across three of them and was able to closely inspect one example. I was not disappointed.

Kretschmer wrote his review in the December 2002 issue of *Sailing* and commented: "The CS 36 is that rare combination, satisfying to race locally, capable of winning its class in the Bermuda or Mackinac races, and tough enough for serious bluewater cruising."

Bill Sandiferm, in his article for *Good Old Boat* (January/ February 2002), was equally effusive: "The Canadian Sea-craft 36 is one of the best-built boats I have yet sailed." The boat used a combination of hull liners and excellent bulkhead tabbing to achieve superb hull rigidity. A Raymond Wall design (Camper and Nicholson), the deep-draft version has a fin keel of just over 6 feet in draft, and a spade rudder, which made for nimble handling. There was also a later "Merlin" version that was 2,000 pounds lighter and had a shorter rig, but experienced cruisers have favored the "traditional" version by quite a wide margin. Only about a hundred of the Merlins were built.

Because it is a Canadian boat, it may have been tempting to follow the lead of competitor C & C Yachts and use coring throughout the hull, but according to Kretschmer, designer Wall was adamant that the hull be built using a solid glass layup. The rest of the boat is balsa cored, so a prepurchase survey checking for delamination will be essential. But these models seem to have held up pretty well provided a previous owner did not go too crazy with the cordless drill he got for Christmas.

When I looked over the CS 36, I was struck by how contemporary the boat looks despite being designed over thirty years ago. There is no exterior teak, it has

a beautiful keel-stepped double-spreader rig, and there are only moderate overhangs ending in a reverse transom. In fact if you can find one for sale that has been in freshwater all its life (and there are many on the Great Lakes), it might be difficult to convince anyone that your new acquisition dates from a 1970s drawing board.

Down below, handholds and storage are well planned, with exceptionally high aluminum fiddles in the galley making it impossible for that bowl of chili to fly off the countertop. The settee apparently came in either a fixed or foldup version, the latter being similar to that found on the Islander 36. On the boat I saw, a foldup double was cleverly designed into the dinette and obviously very comfortable. The interior plan is otherwise fairly standard, with the ubiquitous quarter berth to starboard and

Years Produced	1978–1987 (Traditional)
Designer	Raymond Wall
Estimated Hulls Produced	290
Length Overall	36 feet 6 inches
Length at Waterline	29 feet 3 inches
Draft (shoal/deep keel)	4 feet 11 inches/6 feet 3 inches
Beam	11 feet 6 inches
Sail Area	640 square feet
Capsize Number	1.8
Sail Area/Displacement Ratio	16.5
Displacement/Length Ratio	277
Displacement	15,500 lbs.
Ballast	6,500 lbs.
Typical Engine	Westerbeke 30 hp
Fuel Capacity	35 gallons
Water Capacity	83 gallons
Typical Price Range	$40,000–$50,000 USD
Most Active Owners Association	www.closereach.com/csoa/cs36

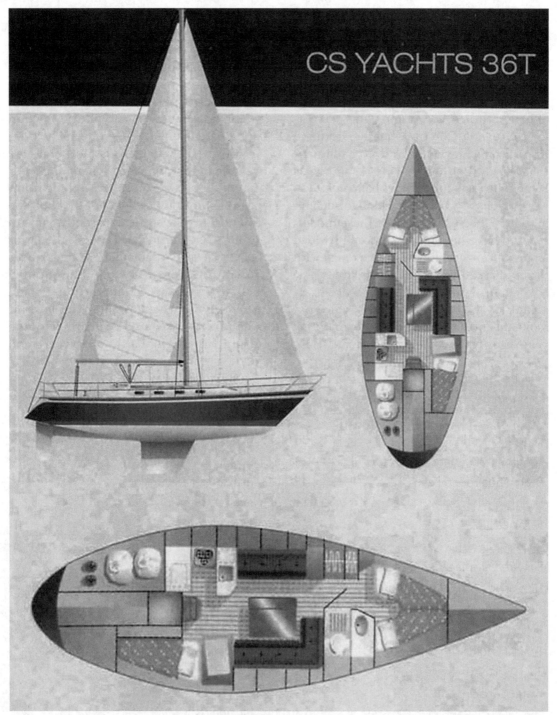

The Canadian Sailcraft Traditional layout is just that—traditional. The boat is perfect for a couple. What sets it apart is the build quality. (Courtesy Mike Wilcox/CS Owners' Association)

a nav station available via the same area. Having the engine tucked under the cockpit did allow for a more commodious interior, but access is therefore only modest. The head, however, is nicely sized, and using it for showers and extended living aboard is certainly feasible.

Since I was unable to sail on this design, I was happy to come across a review of the CS 36 written by Duncan Kent in the British sailing magazine *Sailing Today*. Apparently the CS 35 and 36 were imported to Britain for quite a while in the 1980s, and the article from the September 2007 issue is well illustrated. You can link to the article as a PDF file at http://closereach.com/csoa/sailingtodaycs36.pdf

Kent actually test-sailed a 1982 version and reported that the boat handled well on a blustery day with winds up to 30 knots. The rudder gets some support from a bustle faired into the stern, and is deep enough to provide a solid bite. All lines from the masthead are led aft, and a traveler just forward of the companionway makes for easy mainsail trimming. The T-cockpit does not seem dated, and in all the reviews nothing negative was noted about either gelcoat cracking or soggy decks on these cored boats.

I generally prefer a classic trunk cabin that has at least a 70 degree angle to the side deck. Other more racy coachroofs as on the Islander 36 and Newport 41 are sleeker, but I have always liked being able to brace my foot against a trunk cabin when going forward, such as on the Niagara and Morgan. And of course it makes for a natural bench seat, depending on the handrail location that may be a pain in the – – –. The slotted aluminum toe rail on the CS is not as secure as the 5-inch bulwark on the Morgan 382, but it is certainly very

functional. If you convert to a slutter or a cutter rig, the toe rail allows an easy anchor point for running backstays, which stiffen the rig for sailing to weather.

As mentioned, although the hull is solid fiberglass, the deck, coachroof, and cockpit sole are balsa cored. Careful inspection as always is needed in these areas. In addition, gate valves were standard from the factory. If they have not already been upgraded, they should be changed over to quality ball valves.

These boats also came standard with an Isomat anodized spar. Painted spars are a maintenance headache; they will have paint bubbling up around the fittings no matter how careful you may be with priming and applying linear polyurethane spray paint. I have seen Isomat spars that are twenty-five years old and still look very good, requiring only an occasional "wash and wax."

But the big thing on this boat is the build quality. I especially like the fact that overhead composite battens were used instead of a fiberglass liner, so that if new wiring needs to be run, it is not a complete impossibility. Wall even allowed for a recessed toe space in the galley so that one could brace as close as possible to the countertop—something else I have never seen before.

The Good, the Bad, and the Ugly

I was unable to find an example of the CS 36 that had circumnavigated, whereas I found at least five examples of the Islander 36 that have done so. But considering that about three times as many Islanders were built than the Canadian Sailcraft, and the CS factory was on the Great Lakes, this is not really surprising. There was one CS

Arbutus Girl *is a 1984 CS 36T lovingly cared for by owner Brian Shaw. Note the elegant dodger, stowed bimini, and wide side decks for safe transits forward. The in-mast furling was an aftermarket addition.* (Courtesy Brian Shaw)

36 in my marina that had sailed the South Pacific. I have little doubt that this design will hold up offshore.

Clearly the most important negative item is the difficult access to the engine. Of course it is also true that one can go many months without needing to touch a good diesel, but if you have one of the originals that is now thirty years old, you might need to get hands-on more often. And a V drive generally reduces output horsepower to the propeller by 15 percent. Designer Ray Wall was kind enough to reply to my e-mail query and agreed that this was maybe the one thing he regrets, saying ". . . your negative observation on the engine access is not the first. What at the time seemed a good idea, using a V drive, resulted in the service points ending up at the wrong end of the compartment. I certainly learnt my lesson on that one."

On my comparisons list in the Appendices, I have rated this boat number one as to build quality. But although it is better built than, say, the Islander or the Hunter, described in other chapters, you may have to pay perhaps twice as much as those two examples. The CS 36 does not look dated even in a slip next to many of today's designs, and is a candidate worthy of consideration for coastal or bluewater cruising.

Owner Comments

Brian Shaw of British Columbia owns *Arbutus Girl*, a 1984 CS 36, and reports like others that the design is very accommodating in higher wind speeds:

"On my first sail with her we hit 25- to 30-knot winds and she behaved as if she relished the conditions. In fact she doesn't really hit her stride until the winds are at least 10 to 15 knots. These boats are great sailors."

The Freedom 36 Hard Earned going to weather. Note the "camberspar" sleeved into the jib to give it better sail shape. The unstayed rig does not allow for much forestay tension, which is partially offset with the camberspar innovation. (Courtesy owner William Cormack)

Freedom 36

When Garry Hoyt first came out with his amazing Freedom 40, I was just learning how to sail. As I looked at a promotional photo showing the boat charging along on a reach, I was struck by how much sense everything made, at least to me. Ready to tack? Just turn the wheel. Need to bear off and run before the wind? Just ease out the wishbone booms and let the cat ketch rig do its thing. On top of it all was a fascinating center cockpit design and sweeping lines that people seemed to either love or hate. I was one of the lovers.

Freedom Yachts were first built at the highly regarded Tillotson Pearson yard, but in 1989 Everett Pearson sold the division. The boats were then built in a facility dedicated to just the Freedom brand. Once Gary Mull was brought on board, they went to a more traditional sail plan, but they still used freestanding carbon fiber spars. The Freedom 36/38 by Mull was one of the most popular designs, incorporating a small jib that depended on a sleeved "camberspar" to help with pointing when going to weather. Taking advantage of the lack of any obstructing backstay, all Freedoms designed by Mull have big roaches on the mainsail. You could even opt for a Hoyt "Gunmount" spinnaker pole, which allowed you to set and

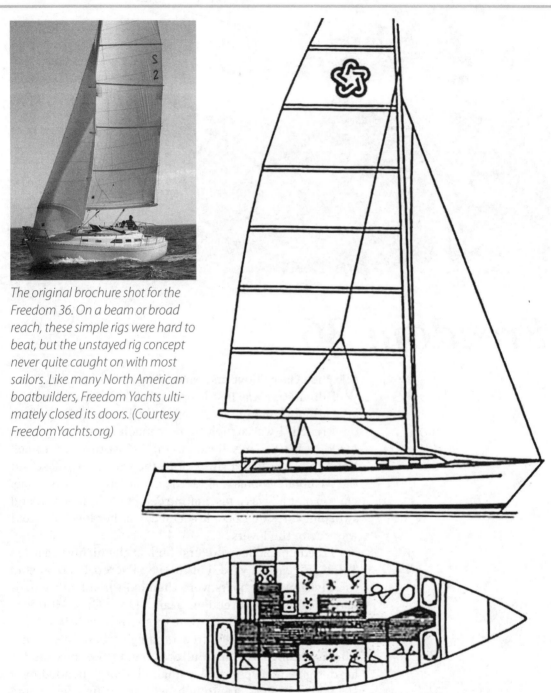

The original brochure shot for the Freedom 36. On a beam or broad reach, these simple rigs were hard to beat, but the unstayed rig concept never quite caught on with most sailors. Like many North American boatbuilders, Freedom Yachts ultimately closed its doors. (Courtesy FreedomYachts.org)

The wide beam of the Freedom 36 makes for an impressive head compartment and sizeable aft berth. Note the extremely simple unstayed rig and slightly offset companionway, which affords easier access to the aft berth. (Courtesy FreedomYachts.org)

Years Produced	1985–1991
Designer	Gary Mull
Estimated Hulls Produced	200
Length Overall	36 feet 4 inches
Length at Waterline	30 feet 5 inches
Draft (shoal/deep keel)	4 feet 6 inches/6 feet
Beam	12 feet 5 inches
Sail Area	685 square feet (sloop)
Capsize Number	2.06
Sail Area/Displacement Ratio	18.5
Displacement/Length Ratio	228
Displacement	14,370 lbs.
Ballast	6,500 lbs.
Typical Engine	Yanmar 3GM30
Fuel Capacity	35 gallons
Water Capacity	65 gallons
Typical Price Range	$40,000–$55,000 USD
Owners Association(s)	www.freedomyachts.org

deploy a relatively small chute from the cockpit. For novice sailors, these designs were as approachable and user-friendly as sailboats can get. A few 36s were built using the cat ketch rig that Hoyt had reintroduced to the sailing world on his 40, but the majority of the 36s were sloops.

These boats love reaching in winds over 10 knots and are easy to sail to weather, but pointing ability does suffer due to the lack of a true headsail on a tensioned forestay. However, probably nobody knows these boats better than Mark Edwards, an original factory broker with nearly thirty years' experience on the Freedom line. He has sailed the 36/38 extensively. He commented:

"There were I believe 155 Freedom 36/38s built between 1986 and 1992. About seven or eight were cat ketch, and after 1989 they were all 38 feet with the swim step extension. You could also buy a fiberglass extension to turn your 36 into a 38. For me the rig is the big selling point on these boats. Unfortunately, sailors are a pretty conservative bunch, and we were never able to change the industry as a whole. But the Freedom 36 rig is very robust. It always surprises me that people will fly cross-country in a plane with a wing that no longer uses stays, but they hesitate to try an unstayed rig. The rig has no failure points like conventional stayed boats. A Freedom 45 has circumnavigated twice with the same type rig."

Edwards went on to describe how he and a friend took a 36 out on Narragansett Bay on a Force 5 January day with the goal of breaking the mast.

"We slam-gybed the boat repeatedly in over 30 knots of wind and she took it every time. And if you are running dead downwind with this rig, your margin of error is much bigger since it has no obstructing stays and you can wing the mast out 90 degrees to the hull. Even an all-standing gybe is not a big problem with this rig."

As of this writing, the new Boeing Dreamliner is in production with a wing that has to accept stress loads much greater than the typical cruising sailboat mast. And the construction material? Carbon fiber—and no stays like those old planes!

The Freedom 36 is included here not just for the rig but also the overall build quality and a spacious interior. In fact, at a whopping 12 feet 5 inches of beam in 36 feet, she has more beam than any of the other designs reviewed in this book.

Not surprisingly this makes for a lot of elbow room, to include the best quarter cabin you will find on a 36-footer. Teak veneers, battens, and accents were used throughout, giving the cabin a cozy feel not typical of boats in this size or price range. The settee is full beam, the head is unusually spacious, and the dinette can be completely folded up against the forward bulkhead.

This boat is balsa cored on both the hull and deck, so the usual caveats and warnings apply. It is especially important to check the area where the mast penetrates the coachroof since chafing or stress can occur here. But as with C & C Yachts to the north, Tillotson Pearson Inc. (TPI) in Rhode Island had a lot of experience in building cored boats when they built the 36. The majority are still out there with no delamination issues. Indeed for me the

only real negative in buying a cored boat is that major hull or deck repairs require more skill than with solid layup boats, so you want to buy one that is sound, and keep it that way. Use particular care when installing new deck through-hulls.

The Good, the Bad, and the Ugly

The Freedom 36 has a big interior and excellent build quality with nice use of teak below. This does not look like a plastic Tupperware boat. The standard engine was the dependable Yanmar 3GM30, one of the best sail auxiliaries ever made.

Serious cruisers may not like the difficulty in repairing a cored hull in the event of a collision or grounding. When going to weather, some owners commented that the windage from the large-diameter mast plus a small jib hurt pointing ability, especially on shoal-draft models.

Sailing downwind, the big main is easily winged out for running and has no chafing issues on this unstayed rig, but flying a large conventional genoa is not possible with the fractional rig. You are limited to either flying a spinnaker or jib top reacher that will probably not be masthead height, making it smaller and easier to handle but also affording less sail area.

The rare cat ketch version of this boat should be better downwind and quite handsome, in my opinion. I have never sailed one, but some online comments mention that the bow will bury fairly easily due to the weight of the mast at the extreme forward position on the hull.

Owner Comments

"As I became older, I did want a reliable boat that I can easily sail singlehanded when necessary. I bought the F38 in Rhode Island in 2004 and sailed her to

Europe via the Azores. We met a storm with winds up to 60 knots. We were running under a bare pole before the wind using the autopilot. The boat behaved wonderfully. When the wind lessened we were hit in the night by a freak wave and were thrown on our beam, which bent the masthead slightly sideways. There was hardly any water in the boat, and she righted and we finished the trip without any problem. Later I used her to cruise the Atlantic coast of France, renowned for its tides, up to 40 feet, and currents than can exceed 10 knots. Not a problem there. I sailed about 11K miles with her. Because I like the concept so much, we also bought in 2008 a 45-foot Freedom *(also a Mull design). This boat is in the Caribbean; we sail her in the winter and have done 8K miles with her so far. We sail the 38-footer in the summer in the Netherlands.*

"Having seen many different types of boats, I like the Freedoms very much. They're built to a high-quality standard with stiffer hulls then I sometimes have seen in Europe with cheaper popular mass-production boats. The Freedoms are easy to handle in adverse conditions. I wonder why they are not more popular among the cruising community."

—Hans Hansen, owner of both a
Freedom 38 and 45

Moondance *is an Islander 36 that was overhauled and cruised by owners Conor and Lanea Riley. This is a 1981 version sailing thirty years later at Channel Islands National Park. (Courtesy Conor Riley)*

Islander 36

The Islander 36 is one of the most popular 36-footers ever produced; nearly all 900 of them were built at the Costa Mesa, California, factory. The boat acquired a remarkable reputation and following over the years, with lines that still warrant a second glance forty years after leaving the drawing board.

Anyone needing testimony as to the seakeeping abilities of this design can look to July 16, 2009, when Zac Sunderland arrived in Los Angeles, California, after circumnavigating on his 1972 Islander *Intrepid*. He had purchased the boat for less than $10,000 and took just thirteen months to tie the knot on his 27-year-old vessel. And oh by the way, he was 17 years old when he did it.

Another I-36 named *Pakele* also circumnavigated, and at least a dozen have made passages from the West Coast to the South Pacific. And while the fixer-upper that Zac Sunderland bought had an unusually low starting price (after the initial purchase), he spent a considerable sum to renovate *Intrepid*. Virtually all Islander 36s on the used market will be considerably below $50,000. This will allow some room for any needed gear and outfitting.

The Islander 36 was an Alan Gurney design originally intended to be an IOR racer-cruiser. Gurney had designed the legendary *Windward Passage*, and with a 40 percent ballast to displacement ratio he did not intend for the I-36 to be a slouch. Although certainly fast, it became better known as a performance cruiser with timeless lines that still turn heads to this day. Noted naval architect Robert Perry summed it up admirably:

"It was not performance that put the I-36 on the map. It was style spelled Joe Artese. He was the designer whom Islander hired to design the interior and deck of the I-36. Joe had not been involved exclusively in sailing yacht design projects, and the result of this was that he brought to the project a fresh approach to the interior layout. The interior of the I-36 was a true breakthrough . . . it had the most open interior yet seen. There was strong attention given to comfort and the integration of interior components."

The 36 had a cleverly done saloon table that folded up completely against the bulkhead when not in use. When the table was stowed, the entire interior beam of the boat was available to stretch out. But this was just one of many refinements and attention to detail that made the boat just as pleasing forty years after it first came out in 1971. It may well be that this enduring appeal is what put Islander out of business. As older boats came on the used market at lower and lower prices, potential new boat clients were lost. Ultimately the Islander molds were sold to Newport Offshore Yachts in 1986.

At a time when many designs intended for club racing had fin keels and spade rudders, the I-36 was given a skeg-supported rudder. This has proven to enhance tracking downwind and the overall strength of the critical rudder-hull interface. The

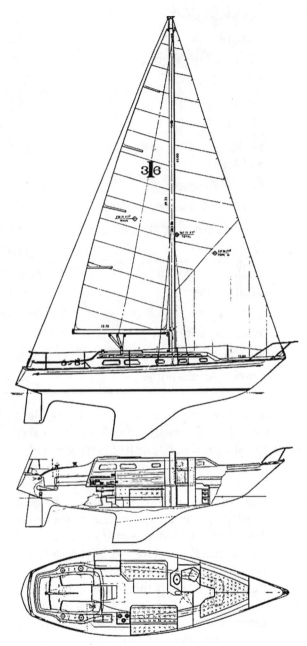

The I-36 was an elegant Alan Gurney design with the interior detail by Joe Artese. The skeg rudder, keel-stepped mast, and double-spreader rig all add up to strength combined with performance. Only the earliest boats had the tiller as shown. (Courtesy Islander 36 Association)

Years Produced	1971–1986
Designer	Alan Gurney/Joe Artese
Estimated Hulls Produced	880
Length Overall	36 feet
Length at Waterline	28 feet 4 inches
Draft (shoal/deep keel)	6 feet
Beam	11 feet 2 inches
Sail Area	576 square feet
Capsize Number	1.8
Sail Area/Displacement Ratio	16
Displacement/Length Ratio	264
Displacement	13,450 lbs.
Ballast	5,820 lbs.
Typical Engine	Pathfinder 42 hp /Yanmar 30 hp
Fuel Capacity	32 gallons
Water Capacity	54 gallons
Typical Price Range	$18,000–$40,000 USD
Owners Association(s)	www.islander36.org

boat balances well, and the strong class racing at places like San Francisco Bay has shown that even after forty years this boat can sail with, or even by, the latest racer-cruisers coming onto the market. The twin-spreader rig has shown to be a quality installation over the years other than some mast-step corrosion issues and occasional chainplate issues (see below). The deck design was done by Joe Artese and included such things as angled cockpit wells for sailing while heeled, recessed genoa tracks (later models), and a proper traveler for mainsail trim.

One thing to watch for is a failing overhead liner. Most years this was a heavy vinyl system that had zippered openings to the sides, and repairing or replacing these is difficult. Since most of these boats are over 30 years old, you will have to find one that was lovingly maintained to justify tapping this design as your cruising home. There are some good ones still out there, but finding them will take awhile.

The 36 has a tremendous owners association, www.islander36.org, with the best upgrade and maintenance details of any website out there. These owners love their boats, with the biggest concentration being on San Francisco Bay. Just be aware that many of these boats are now at 40 years of age and counting, and it may not be cost-effective to repair or reinforce problem areas to make them ready for offshore use.

The Good, the Bad, and the Ugly

Diesel engine models are a must. The earliest production years had Palmer and

Atomic 4 gas engines, which would be forty years old by now, so look for later models with the Perkins 4-108 or a more recent repower with other makes.

Sails, like diesels, are expensive, and since this was a popular club racer, there is no reason to settle for a boat with minimal sail inventory. A tired main might be acceptable if the headsails are in good shape, but find value in the sail locker.

Dodgers are also very expensive, but most I-36s seem to have dodgers added to them over the years. So, again, why buy one without a dodger if you can find one that has a dodger installed? Even if the actual canvas is on its last legs, the tubing framework is a valuable addition.

Beyond the baseline of a diesel, dodger, and good sail inventory, everything else is gravy if you buy the base boat at a low enough price. Just remember that "needs cosmetics" is a relative thing. If the whole boat needs an expensive linear polyurethane paint job, you are talking as much as $10,000. Only you can decide what is cosmetically acceptable and, equally important, what jobs can be accomplished with your skill set. Nothing brings a boat's resale value down faster than poorly executed owner paint jobs.

Most experienced surveyors on the West Coast will have looked at a least a few I-36s. If you're buying through a broker, it is advisable not to use a surveyor provided by the broker. He may be fine, but your best bet is to check around and find someone who has surveyed this specific model and is not beholden to the broker for referral business. What follows is a list of items that will need checking.

Blisters were seen on some Islanders, not atypical for many production sailboats of this era. In some cases these were mi-

nor, but in other years (and sometimes in areas of warmer water) the pox was significant enough to merit a gelcoat peel and barrier coating. For those willing to take on the nasty grinding job themselves, real bargains can be had by purchasing a blister boat and then removing all gelcoat below the waterline. After drying out the hull, epoxy or vinylester resin can be used to recoat, reprime, and paint with antifouling. This sort of sweat equity can mean a purchase price of thousands less—if you don't mind grinding fiberglass! If you are lucky, the boat you buy was already properly treated. If not, at least be sure what you may be getting into. A "hang and hold" out-of-the-water survey is usually well worth the expense, and significant issues can be used to negotiate a lower price, assuming you press forward.

Chainplates on some of the earlier model years were not sufficiently anchored, so make sure they are tied in belowdeck with adequate backing. The problem seemed to be confined to the lower shrouds only on this double-spreader rig. Many tips on how to retrofit these chainplates are available at the www.islander36.org website.

Bulkheads and frames on Islanders need careful inspection. This is something that a knowledgeable surveyor will immediately check on this model. The main bulkhead forward by the mast was known for separation where it joined with the hull, so check this and all tabbing carefully.

Check the mast step because in many cases the lowest 6 inches of the mast step corrodes after thirty-plus years of sitting in the bilge. In the event that it has not been done already, the repair is not especially difficult, but it's still a cost factor to reckon with in your purchase decision. The Islander 36 also has a distinctive black anodized aluminum toe rail, and in every one I have seen, the stainless steel bolts are pretty much welded to the toe rail due to electrolysis. In other words, you need to make sure that the toe rail is not leaking excessively because removing it to do a rebed is very difficult. My suggestion is to hose-test the boat for leaks.

Owner Profile, Moondance

Conor and Lanea Riley pulled into Los Cabos, Mexico, just before the thirtieth anniversary of their 1981 Islander 36 *Moondance*. According to their blog, "We are two silly newlyweds who thought it would be a cool idea to buy a boat and sail south to tropical beaches of Mexico and maybe

beyond." Taking less than nine months from purchase to departure, they managed to cram a lot of projects into that time, including a complete repower with a new BetaMarine diesel.

Both Lanea and Conor had a lot of sailing experience on San Francisco Bay plus a few charters in the Caribbean prior to taking the plunge. They had sailed Merit 25s and owned a Ranger 29, so to them the jump up to a 36-footer was actually substantial even if theirs is one of the smaller boats in most cruising anchorages. But the significant difference is that they are both in their early thirties and in great health, so they can take full advantage of their cruising experience.

"Our boat was relatively lightly used," said Conor, "but we still ended up doing

Luna Sea is just one of many Islander 36s on San Francisco Bay, here sailing on a port tack just after clearing the Bay Bridge. With a production run of nearly 900, there are plenty available on the used market. (Courtesy owner Charlie Bergstedt)

a lot of work." The bulkheads were reinforced by adding a second sister bulkhead. Refrigeration and a propane stove were installed, the holding tank was replaced, and the DC lighting was upgraded. Then the checkbook really got tested with all new electronics—radar, chartplotter, depthsounder, AIS, VHF, and new batteries. Finally a windvane was installed—a big expense but one they do not regret. "We love the windvane, and use it a lot," says Lanea.

Moondance represents a boat that had more invested in new cruising gear than the original value of the boat itself. This is not an unusual story, but if care is taken it is still possible to find a good Islander 36 and complete all upgrades without going much over $50,000. The key would be to owner-install as much of the gear as possible, and avoid too many over-the-top invoices for marine technician services. For more on *Moondance*, her upgrades, and her travels, go to svmoondance.wordpress.com and check out their blog.

Additional Owner Comments

"The boat goes well to windward, tracks well downwind with a chute set, and doesn't mind ocean swells. She does not like a short chop with light wind and will pound. Depending on your engine and prop, the boat does 6 to 7 knots, but like many boats it tends to back to port or starboard in reverse. Plan ahead and work with the engine, using light power and patience."

—Rick Van Mell

Mark Schneider's BubbleCuffer *is looking good in her home waters of Maine. Note the shrouds and genoa track well inboard for tight sheeting angles, and just a hint of teak to class her up a bit. A bubblecuffer was a log driver—on the rivers of Maine back when they still had the drives—who was particularly adept at running out on the logs and picking the jams; hence, his cuffs where always in the bubbles. (Courtesy Mark Schneider)*

Pearson 36-2

Pearson Yachts was founded by cousins Everett and Clinton Pearson back in 1956, making them pioneers in fiberglass boatbuilding with models like the Triton 28 and the Alberg 35 (both of which have circumnavigated). It was based in Rhode Island until filing for bankruptcy in 1991. I have seen and surveyed a fair number of Pearsons and feel they offer excellent value, with a build quality and finish level that—while not perfect—improved over the years. In fact if I could somehow reach out and resuscitate just one of the many American sailboat manufacturers that have fallen by the wayside in the last two decades, it would be Pearson Yachts.

There are several Pearson models with production runs long enough to make it into this book, even below the $50,000 price threshold. The 365 is a pretty boat, and I like the raised gunwale and side decks on that model, but the only dedicated sleeping area on her is the V-berth. At least one 365 has circumnavigated, so the boat (which came either as a sloop or the more popular ketch) is a viable candidate. But far more 36-2s were built, and they are deserving of a place here.

The boat came with the option of a fin keel at six feet six inches of draft and a keel centerboard that was just over eight feet with the board down, four feet and change with the board up. The centerboard housing is nicely integrated into the dinette. For those wanting the ability to tuck into shallow coves, it is nice to have this feature without compromising interior space as with other designs.

The 36-2 has an efficient, uncluttered interior typical of Shaw's work. But what makes the boat is the nice quarter cabin to starboard. This coupled with a very respectably sized head to port make for a very sustainable liveaboard and cruising arrangement, especially for 36 feet. Obvi-

Time Out is a Pearson 36-2 not yet decked out with cockpit canvas or cruising gear. But note how the position of the mainsheet traveler makes for an easy dodger installation. (Courtesy owner Gregg Montgomery)

Years Produced	1985–1990
Designer	David Shaw
Estimated Hulls Produced	290
Length Overall	36 feet 6 inches
Length at Waterline	29 feet 7 inches
Draft (shoal/deep keel)	4 feet 4 inches/6 feet 6 inches
Beam	12 feet 4 inches
Sail Area	660 square feet
Capsize Number	1.8
Sail Area/Displacement Ratio	17
Displacement/Length Ratio	259
Displacement	15,000 lbs.
Ballast	5,800 lbs.
Typical Engine	Yanmar 30 hp
Fuel Capacity	22 gallons
Water Capacity	100 gallons
Typical Price Range	$40,000–$50,000 USD
Most Active Owners Association	http://pearsonowners.com

ously whenever you specify a large quarter cabin, the cockpit locker stowage suffers, so some discipline will be needed. Forget about dive tanks or an excessive number of sails, unless you want to use the V-berth as a garage—which is a common outcome.

Other interior details are rarely seen on other boats. One such detail is cubbyhole storage port and starboard in the V-berth, turning wasted space into useful stowage. Also, the toilet is mounted fore-and-aft and close to the boat's centerline, which may seem like a small detail but eliminates worrying about whether you happen to be on a favored tack for using the head. Finally, the settee is truly massive for a boat of this size. The table itself is beautifully done in teak, and although Pearson didn't bother with a dropleaf to extend the table to the portside settee

they didn't have to. There is seating for six with the table just as is. Do you really want more than six over for dinner?

The Good, the Bad, and the Ugly

Perhaps the best way to describe this boat is "refined." It is clear that everything was well thought out by an experienced designer and builder. Maybe the most telling way to see this is to ask how much a contemporary designer would change in this boat if starting from scratch.

The interior layout is fitted as a seagoing galley. The quarter berth—thanks to the beam carried aft—is generous. It came with a direct-drive Yanmar diesel and quality hardware. There is just enough teak to give her some character but not enough to be a maintenance headache. In-

The typical interior of the Pearson 36-2. With just 36 feet of space, designers have to decide what the priorities will be. Note the similarities to the Freedom 36, but instead of a large head compartment, designer Bill Shaw opted for a larger galley.

stalling a dodger is not difficult. The hull layup was excellent and has held up well over the years.

Most owners would agree that there is little ugly about the Pearson 36-2. My only advice would be to pick the deep-draft version if possible, although Greg Swedish writes below that he is very happy with his centerboard version.

Owner Comments

Greg Swedish owns *Four the Soul*, hull number 101, and cruises it primarily in the Northeast.

"The layout of the P36-2 is great. We sleep in the aft berth and just this past year had a custom mattress made. The front V-berth is used as our 'closet.' The galley is good and well positioned in the boat; we love to cook, and the provided stove/ oven works great. In regards to sailing ability, she loves to drop her shoulder and point. We have the shoal keel with centerboard, which we love. It makes going into shallow coves so much easier. The cockpit is great, with the seats slightly pitched, making them very comfortable as well as not dumping people when the boat heels. We have added stern rail seats, which are also great. We had searched for many boats of the mid to late 1980s vintage. Because we had two kids in college, money was an issue. From all the boats we saw, the P36-2 had the best layout and looks. We wanted to have the privacy of the 'three-cabin' layout in case we did bring people overnight. We were not fans of the open quarter berth or the folding aft doors (Catalina 36) that most boats of similar size had. One of the problems with the design is that the deck jib track holds water. So if that's not properly taken care of (rebed every five or so years), water will get into the core, as was the case with mine. The decks were in poor shape, but my wife and I loved the layout and the price was right."

—Greg Swedish, hull #101,
Four the Soul

Jazz, a 1978 CSY 37, anchored at Green Turtle Key, Abaco, Bahamas. Note the cutter rig, flush deck, and excellent ventilation via large opening hatches. Not a rocketship under sail but strong and salty looking. (Courtesy owner Peter Hibbard)

CSY 37

The pundits out there will, of course, find fault with at least some of the choices included in this book, including this one. The three finalists for the last slot on The List were the Valiant 32, the Catalina 38, and the Caribbean Sailing Yachts (CSY) 37. The Valiant is a great boat, but unfortunately even those that have had complete blister repairs have, on occasion, had a reoccurrence once the boat was in the tropics. The Catalina 38 is similar to the Newport 41 but not as spacious, and I really wanted to go a different way with my last selection. It would have been very easy to write about yet another racer-cruiser from the 1970s, or another Taiwanese double-ender that made it under the $50,000 barrier. So the CSY gets the nod, for specific reasons that follow. But the real reason is, quite frankly, that I have a soft spot for any boat that dares to be different.

The CSY is, to be sure, a boat that people seem to either love or hate. Some call it aesthetically challenged; others like myself are happy to see a designer who is willing to take a chance. A semi-flush deck that opens up the interior and allows for easy dinghy stowage on top? Nice change. A Pullman berth on the B interior with the head in the forepeak, allowing for a huge main saloon? Interesting approach. Engine access in the cockpit via a huge hatch instead of wedged below under the companionway? Cool.

This is not a boat that will win any races or tack through 70 degrees. But if you want a Cadillac ride and are willing to be one of the last boats to make the next anchorage, there are some offsetting features to this design that are worth a look.

CSY Yachts was the brainchild of retired dentist Jack Van Ost, who loved sailing the Caribbean and realized that others wanted to vacation there on sailboats like he did. He essentially invented the lease-back concept, whereby a private party purchases a new boat and then enters it into the CSY charter fleet. This leveraged Van Ost's capital, and his fleet quickly grew to dominate the market, although imitators followed.

Van Ost tried getting his boats built by various established yards such as Pearson and Irwin, but he ultimately decided to invest in a state-of-the-art factory of his own near Tampa, Florida. For about a decade the company could barely keep up with the demand, selling directly to the client without a dealer network.

Every single boat included on The List has some shortcomings, even my favorite—the Golden Wave 42. But there is one thing that the CSY 37 does not suffer from, and that is a lack of structural strength for offshore work, perhaps because it was designed by a relative amateur who erred on the side of caution in his layup specifications. Peter Schmitt had worked with Bill Tripp but was not actually a naval architect himself. He met with Van Ost, was added to the team, and eventually was assigned to design the 33, 37, and 44.

Years Produced	1978–1981
Designer	CSY Yachts
Estimated Hulls Produced	90
Length Overall	37 feet 3 inches
Length at Waterline	29 feet 2 inches
Draft (shoal/deep keel)	5 feet 5 inches
Beam	12 feet
Sail Area	610 square feet
Capsize Number	1.71
Sail Area/Displacement Ratio	13.2
Displacement/Length Ratio	360
Displacement	22,000 lbs.
Ballast	8,500 lbs.
Typical Engine	Perkins 50 hp diesel
Fuel Capacity	40 gallons
Water Capacity	80 gallons
Typical Price Range	$30,000–$50,000 USD
Most Active Owners Association	www.sailboatowners.net

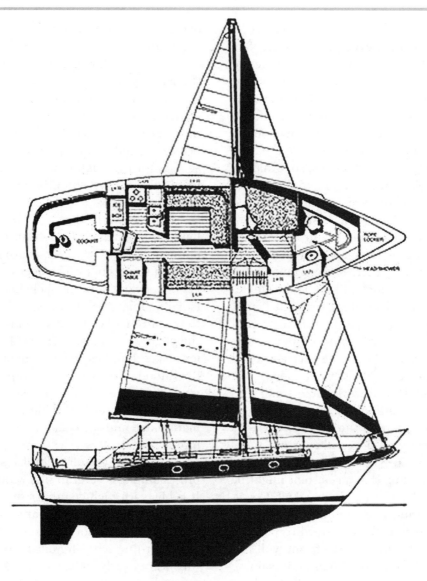

The CSY 37 with the Plan B "Pullman" berth interior, made possible by the unusual location of the head compartment forward. There was also a hard-to-find tall rig option, probably a better choice for lighter Pacific winds.

The 37 weighs nearly 20,000 pounds and has zero coring. When combined with the flush design, the immensely strong hull and deck make for a solid shell that is as close to one piece as you can find. I once saw a plug from a holesaw that had been used to drill a hole in the side of a CSY and it was about ¾ inch thick. If you removed the mast and engine and sealed all the openings shut, I believe you could send this boat over Niagara Falls and expect it to come bobbing out after a minute or two, relatively intact.

Her bigger sister, the CSY 44, was a

huge hit, and the CSY 37 came along soon after—though it never matched the 44's sales numbers. Both were built to take the abuse of the charter trade. They favored big cockpits and engines to ensure that the clients were comfortable and safe. In the late 1970s, the Ericson 39, Pearson 40, and most of the Columbias were creating a wave with their flush decks, so it may be that the CSY 37 was reacting to that trend.

Since the boat was optimized for the charter trade, there was a standard two-cabin version that chopped up the interior. I have not seen it, but on paper I do not care for it. Fortunately there is also a much nicer "B" option that looks like a great single-couple layout. Note, however, that Plan B puts the single head all the way forward. I suppose this is appropriate considering that the word is derived from the old tradition of relieving oneself at the bow, or "head," of a sailing ship. How it works on a small sailboat might be rather interesting, though.

In keeping with the different tweaks on this boat, you descend an almost elegant three-step "staircase" into the cabin. Notwithstanding that a seat belt might be recommended if using the head while sailing to weather, I really like the B layout. The Pullman berth is forward to port, so having the head and stateroom well forward allows for a very open main saloon/galley that has a completely different feel than any other 37-footer I have seen.

Many readers may remember that CSY used a lot of faux teak Formica paneling, and this does detract from the feel of the interior, depending on how much of the original 1970s mobile home look is still present. Some owners, like Peter Hibbard, have done an amazing job of renovating the interior using inexpensive materials. On his boat *Jazz*, Peter simply painted over the faux wood veneers. The results are stunning.

Since charter clients wanted ice for their margaritas, a significant number of the 37s were equipped with engine-driven refrigeration. But the original units would now be thirty years old and hopefully have been replaced on any prospect you might see. As for the engine, the location is not inside the cabin, which is relatively rare on a 37-footer.

It is rarer still that a 37-footer would have an engine (Perkins 4-108) that puts out nearly 50 horsepower, but that was the case on these boats. The access is terrific via the cockpit sole and a big hatch, which isolates noise, smell, fires, or leaks from the cabin. In about five seconds you have the engine completely exposed and ready for inspection. Easy access equals a higher likelihood of preventive maintenance, in my experience. There is a slight exposure risk to salt water if the hatch seal is not maintained and the cockpit is taking water into it.

The cockpit itself will raise some eyebrows amongst veteran bluewater sailors. It is big, with high coamings that give that sense of security that many prefer but could also hold a lot of water in the event of a boarding sea. The offset companionway is not overly wide, so getting too much water down below should be preventable, but the bathtub feel of the cockpit itself will give some sailors pause. The cockpit drains are large, but to see if they are truly adequate, it might be prudent to fill the cockpit with a hose to the level of the companionway, check the time needed to drain, and at least double that time to get an idea of what might happen in offshore conditions. Cockpit drainage could easily be doubled in this boat, however, since there are no accommodations below the cockpit sole.

In terms of sailing, my information is all secondhand, but there seems to be a consensus that the standard rig is adequate if not ideal for Carribbean trade winds, and the rare tall rig version is of course better in light air conditions. The mediocre light air sailing abilities of the standard rig seem confirmed by Peter Hibbard in his owner comments below. The ideal combination for performance would be the deep-draft version along with the taller rig, but since this was a Florida boat, only a handful exist.

The 37 is available nicely equipped for under $40,000. If you give yourself some time, you can certainly find one in Florida. The boat is easily truckable for West Coast buyers, but almost none made it there, perhaps because the flush-decked Ericson Cruising 36 was a local alternative. Although I think the CSY is a neat boat, if I was on the West Coast looking for a cruiser, I would not consider paying to truck it west. It is included here more as an option for East Coast cruisers and especially those needing shallow draft.

The Good, the Bad, and the Ugly

If you like a boat strong enough to hit a log at 6 knots and shrug it off, there is a lot to be said for this overbuilt solid

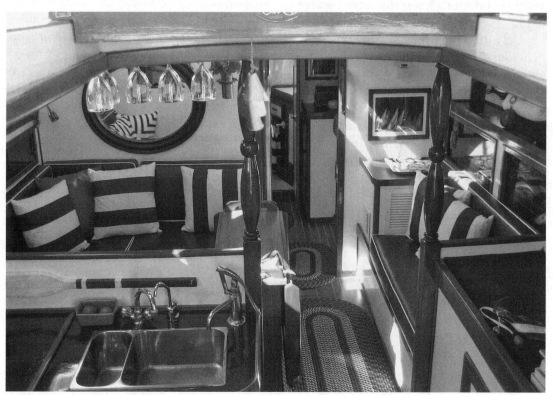

A flush-deck design like the CSY 37 can make for a huge interior. Owner Peter Hibbard took the original dark Formica bulkheads and refinished them for a bright interior worthy of a 40-footer. (Courtesy Peter Hibbard)

glass cruiser. The flush deck makes for a spacious interior. There are lots of deck hatches to ventilate the cabin, and there are easy stowage options for dinghies and kayaks. This is something that I find is continually underestimated. The convenience and safety of easy on-deck dinghy stowage (without affecting sail handling) is something that only experienced cruisers appreciate. Davits are not used by serious cruisers except on larger boats, and the CSY has some great options for deck-stowing a dinghy that can be hoisted aboard via the boom and topping lift. Engine access is superb, with the noise and fluids isolated in a separate compartment out of the accommodations, although care must be taken to keep the hatch watertight.

Ugly, like beauty, is in the eye of the beholder. The flush-deck concept is actually an old one, going back centuries. For owners who tend to go into trawler mode if the wind is not fair, the ample horsepower will be welcome if you want to make progress motorsailing to weather. You will not find a more robust build anywhere, and that counts for a lot if you accidentally park her on a reef and want to have a fighting chance for survival.

Owner Comments

"This boat is very functional, very comfortable for cruising, and a design you can depend on to get you there regardless of the weather. The hull and deck are built of solid fiberglass without a core, which is very rare. Ventilation to the cabin is excellent with many large hatches, which is a great asset in the warmer climates. The one level deck makes traversing at sail and in a sea very safe and easy. Additionally this gives you more usable space below. The solid ¾ keel and skeg-mounted rudder are massive and provide another example of strength and confidence. In my opinion, this is a perfect boat for a couple.

"What I don't like: while the boat sails well off the wind and on a beam or broad reach, it does take about 10 knots to start to really move her. Beating to windward is sometimes a challenge as she does not point that well. Keep in mind this is not a racing design. She was designed for cruising and she does this very well."

—Peter Hibbard, owner of CSY 37 *Jazz*

The perfectly trimmed Hunter 37 Calypso works to weather in Canadian waters. One of the early "Cherubini Hunters," the 37 was cutter rigged. Note the staysail track just forward of the mast. (Courtesy owner Jim Legere)

Hunter 37 Cutter

Hunter Yachts, which filed for bankruptcy in 2012, was for many years the largest manufacturer of sailboats in the United States. For serious bluewater sailors, or perhaps more accurately for online forum rats, Hunter was the boat everybody loved to hate. But Hunter understood that the percentage of sailboat buyers who would be circumnavigating was infinitesimally small, and they marketed themselves accordingly. But in the late 1970s they were starting out with more traditional boats designed by one of the most traditional of designers—John Cherubini.

After interviewing several owners of the Hunter 37 for the book, it quickly became clear that they loved it when someone said, "Boy, your boat doesn't look like a Hunter." And it doesn't. It was designed as a true cutter, with the mast appropriately aft and a foretriangle setup with adequate spacing between stays. Noted designer John Cherubini worked for Hunter Yachts early on, having been retained by owner Warren Luhrs as the head designer. Cherubini designed the 37 in 1977, and the first boat rolled off the production line in 1978. The so-called "Cherubini Hunters" have an avid following and an active owners group.

It is not just the cutter rig that sets this design apart.

On a quiet anchorage after a satisfying sail, Calypso awaits more gunkholing. The Hunter 37 came standard with a self-tending staysail boom, although some owners removed this feature. (Courtesy owner Jim Legere)

Down below, these boats also have surprising headroom, almost 6 feet 4 inches. Many owners comment about the very utilitarian interior design, especially the full shower stall in the head with the washbasin outside, allowing simultaneous access. Aft to port there is a decent double bunk, making this Hunter a good family boat. The well-designed centerline dinette can be left with just the starboard leaf deployed to allow unobstructed access forward but still seat two or three for dining. In fact, the interior design was so finely tuned that there were virtually no significant interior modifications during the eight-year production run.

For potential cruisers probably the most significant variations from one model year to another was in the diesel engine. Beginning in 1980 the standard Yanmar 2QM20 was upgraded to the more appropriate 3QM30. And a few lucky owners with model year 1984 and 1985 had Yanmar 4JHEs installed. Unlike the Yanmar Q series, this was a freshwater-cooled unit,

and could push the boat at hull speed even into a 3-foot chop.

Many owners testified to the sailing qualities of their boat, especially with respect to a balanced helm to weather: "The best thing about this boat is the way she sails: solid, stable and well balanced," says owner Jim Legere. "Lock the wheel and she will happily go to weather all day by herself. The relatively heavy displacement makes for a very comfortable ride—think Cadillac or Lincoln Continental. Off the wind, she can fly! We have seen 9½ knots at times, sliding along the swells on a breezy broad reach. She can reel off the miles on a passage."

The deep-draft Hunter 37 still draws only 5 feet 6 inches, so there are few harbors that will be off-limits to these owners. Ultimate stability will be slightly better with the deep keel, and the boat will likely point a few degrees higher. Of course East Coast owners spending a lot of time on the Intracoastal Waterway or in the Bahamas may want the shoal-draft model.

As far as negatives that have appeared over the years, the two most significant are probably some rudder and deck core issues. The factory did not install an upper rudder shaft bearing, and while this may be tolerable for day sailing, anyone contemplating serious cruising should review the excellent retrofits executed by various 37 owners to strengthen the rudder. Early model years had some reports of oilcanning (flexing) on the cabintop and at the topsides in the V-berth area (see owner comments below). In particular, due to a plywood core on the deck, any poorly bedded fittings could lead to migrating rot and a serious and expensive fix. This is why on this model it would be imperative to have the boat surveyed prior to purchase, preferably by a surveyor familiar with this design.

Other issues such as corrosion at the base of the keel-stepped mast are common on many boats—and a fairly easy repair. However, if the deck and rudder are showing any issues, it is imperative that you factor this into your final decision. If you are a prospective buyer and are on the fence after finding a bargain boat with some issues, you may take comfort in the fact that these designs have a strong owners association. Nearly all the maintenance and structural issues have already been diagnosed, written about, and posted on the owners' forum.

The Good, the Bad, and the Ugly

Overall this boat has a great interior layout, is a true cutter, and a Yanmar diesel

Years Produced	1978–1986
Designer	John Cherubini
Estimated Hulls Produced	403
Length Overall	37 feet
Length at Waterline	30 feet
Draft (shoal/deep keel)	4 feet/5 feet 6 inches
Beam	11 feet 10 inches
Sail Area	710 square feet
Capsize Number	1.81
Sail Area/Displacement Ratio	17
Displacement/Length Ratio	294
Displacement	17,800 lbs.
Ballast	7,100 lbs.
Mast Height Above Water	50 feet
Typical Engine	Yanmar 27 hp
Fuel Capacity	44 gallons
Water Capacity	100 gallons
Typical Price Range	$25,000–$40,000 USD
Owners Association(s)	www.sailboatowners.com/hunter

was standard. Some owners mentioned that the cockpit is too small. If any deck leaks were not addressed in a timely manner, the plywood deck core could rot extensively. It is possible to find these boats under $35,000 in acceptable condition. The deep-keel version is a better bluewater choice, and post-1981 model years are preferable.

Owner Comments

"The cutter rig was new to us when we bought this boat; after ten years we have to say we are cutter converts! It is a great rig for shorthanded sailing. We especially like the club-footed staysail (except downwind in light airs when it flops around a bit). Basically, once the wind gets above 25 knots or so, we just roll in the Yankee jib and sail on the staysail—that is the first reef. At this point, the boat becomes totally self-tending during tacking. This is a very easy boat to solo sail, even in heavy weather. I have been out alone in 35 knots plus."

—Jim Legere, owner of *Calypso*, hull #308

"I installed 2 × 2 vertical stiffeners in the V-berth every six inches. This eliminated the oilcanning in the V-berth. I changed the standing rigging to ⅜" discontinuous rod and added stays from the spreaders to the original attachment points where the running backstays attached to the mast. I replaced all the ports with Lewmar aluminum ones (the six large ones open out, which means that heavy boarding seas just force them to shut tighter). I replaced the cast Bomar hatches with Lewmar aluminum ones. I sealed the mast with Spartite. I replaced the pedestal drive chain with one that is 6 inches longer, and I got rid of the mainsheet sys-

tem and winch and replaced it with a Harken 7:1 to the bridgedeck. I replaced the roller furling with Harken, and replaced the traveler with a Harken line control. I have sailed the boat in 80+ and survived a pitchpole in 1981. After 34 years of bluewater ocean racing, including four TransAtlantics, three Mexico races, and two Antigua race weeks, there is no place I would not feel safe taking the boat. Yes things break. Yes I am always chasing leaks (my crew refers to the starboard settee as the waterboarding bunk). But the real key is maintaining and upgrading. No 30-year-old original boat is going to be safe to cross an ocean. But I guarantee mine is."

—Blaise Warren, original owner since 1980 of *Midnight Sun*, hull #42

"I believe these old Hunters offer great value to those with the time and ability to bring them up to scratch. The design pedigree is impeccable; John Cherubini was one of the most respected American naval architects of his generation. The structure of these old Hunters can only be described as solid. The hull is thick glass: ½ inch below the hull-to-deck joint and more than an inch at the keel stub. (I determined this while installing and replacing through-hulls.) The deck and house are cored with marine plywood. Some owners have had to replace core damaged by seal failure on deck fittings, but I have been lucky. The hull-to-deck joint is bedded in 5200 or similar and bolted through the toe rail every 6 inches." The rudder has been a problem for some, especially after a grounding. My surveyor noted cracks in the skin of mine, so I replaced it. The rig is a heavy Kenyon section, single spreader, with lots of redundancy in the stays and shrouds.

The Hunter 37 layout includes a true aft cabin complete with a door—excellent for privacy but a bit harder to ventilate in the tropics.

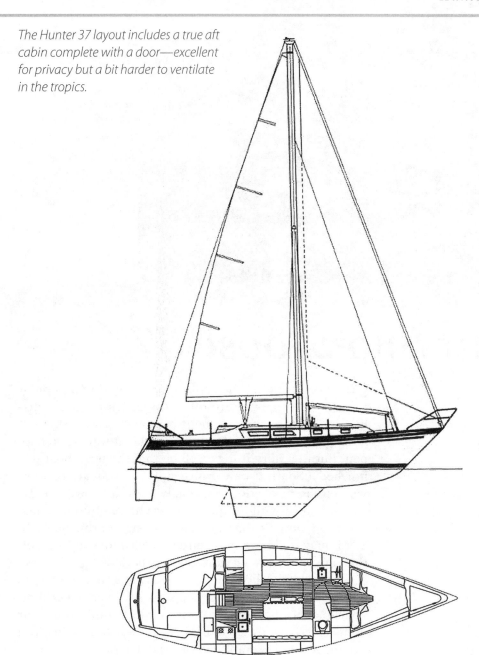

All the major 'bits' for the Hunter 37 cutter, from rig to rudder, are still available in the United States. In my slightly biased opinion, there is not a better value 37-foot sailboat in the North American market."

—Jim Legere, owner of Calypso, hull #308

Mei Wenti, *an example of the conservatively designed Snowgoose 37, is far more likely to safely circumnavigate than it is to capsize. (Courtesy owner Peter Hoggins)*

Prout Snowgoose 37

Boaters observing the sailboats anchored in a popular cruising stopover are often too quick to judge, dismissing a funky ferro-cement boat as unseaworthy or a strange-looking catamaran as an accident waiting to happen. But in reality it may well be that the ferro boat just finished a South Pacific cruise and the catamaran a four-year circumnavigation. Especially if it is a Snowgoose 37, which almost without question has more circumnavigations to its credit than any other design in this book. In fact it may well have more circumnavigations to its credit than any other production sailboat, period.

It would also be a mistake to assume that the Snowgoose should not be included in a book with an upper-limit boat budget of $50,000. With over 500 built and their numbers concentrated in Europe and North America, you can indeed find examples in the $50,000 range. They may be 25 years old, need rewiring, and have a Volvo made by Elves from a converted Peugeot taxi engine, but they are out there. Since these boats were made with solid layup construction, the issues are rarely structural, and with some sweat equity a neglected model can be brought back to life. In researching this book, I found four examples under $50,000 with just a little hunting. One of them seemed intact and ready to go.

Roland and Francis Prout were the Wright brothers of catamaran development. Working from the unlikely location of Canvey Island, England, in the 1950s the two took what was originally a Polynesian concept and applied fiberglass boatbuilding techniques to increasingly larger designs. Their earliest small boats were fast enough to impress in local racing, but the Snowgoose that came along later was clearly a cruising boat with a fairly yacht-like interior finish.

As someone who has built and cruised two cold-molded multihulls, I will admit that, at least to me, the Snowgoose is aesthetically challenged. It has a solid bridgedeck, which helps with rigidity and strength but adds weight, a narrow beam that allows for marina docking but reduces overall space, and a nacelle underwing to allow for headroom in the saloon. The mast and mainsail are so far aft that they seem an afterthought. But the boat has a cruising pedigree that quite frankly is second to none. I have seen them in ports around the world, and although the boat may not tug at everyone's heartstrings as far as looks, their track record begs further investigation.

MULTIHULL STABILITY

A multihull? Offshore? But these boats are more stable upside down than right side up (true)! One gust of wind over 35 knots and a cruising catamaran will flip (untrue)!

As someone who has owned a 50-foot catamaran and also built two smaller trimarans, let me start by making the distinction between the "Win or Capsize" racing multihulls—which can and do capsize due to wind alone—and the much more conservative sail plans and speeds of cruising catamarans. The Snowgoose, for instance, has such a conservative sail plan that any capsize would almost certainly be wave induced. But with a modicum of common sense in heavy seas, even this is unlikely.

In the 1994 Queen's Birthday Storm north of New Zealand, the 38-foot catamaran *Ramtha* (a Roger Simpson design) was caught out with about a dozen boats in seas that reached a verified 40 feet and winds that measured 70 knots. One monohull was lost with all hands; several others rolled and the crews sustained serious injuries. *Ramtha* had been having steering issues even before the storm hit, and ultimately felt they needed to accept the offer by a freighter to take them off

in horrendous conditions. The boat was left to fend for itself.

A week later the owners heard that *Ramtha* had been found upright and intact by another cruiser. When they flew out, they found her still useable, and took her back to Australia to continue her voyaging career. The boat had ridden out several days of some of the worst seas imaginable, lying ahull for the last part of the storm completely uncrewed.

In my experience a cruising boat is more likely to hit something that will hole her rather than encounter a survival storm scenario. In the case of floating things that go bump in the night, multihulls have the huge advantage of reserve buoyancy. Hole one hull and the other(s) will keep her afloat indefinitely. If you hole a monohull, well, the clock starts running.

Multihulls do not have a "capsize number" calculation because these boats depend on form stability rather than ballast to stay upright. A conservatively sailed cruising multihull can be taken offshore, or even all the way around. If they were less costly to build or to fit into marinas, in my opinion at least half the boats out there would be multihulls.

Three private bunk areas and level sailing make the Snowgoose popular for family cruising. Note how far aft the mast is stepped on this headsail-driven design. (Courtesy Prout Yachts)

It was a Prout design that, in 1964, became the first multihull to go around. The Snowgoose came along about a decade later and was probably the most user-friendly, non-intimidating boat built at that time. Neophytes heading out on a test sail found that they didn't have to heel over and spill their coffee when under way. In the cockpit, all halyards and sheets were led aft, and no sail was bigger than an easily managed 300 square feet. Most were cutter rigged; when the wind got up you could furl the jib from the cockpit and use the main and staysail safely in up to 35 knots of wind. And as with most multihulls, the boat was virtually unsinkable—not a small thing when you are sailing at night offshore and are awakened by a loud bump from somewhere forward.

There is a distinction to be made between the Snowgoose and the Snowgoose Elite, which replaced it after 1986. The Elite has a foot more beam and a tad more draft, with the outboard-hung rudders replaced by skeg-hung versions still strong enough to take an intentional beaching. With the added beam, the Elite is a bit more roomy inside, but the sailing characteristics are essentially unchanged. If you are trying to find one of these boats for under $50,000, you will have to consider the older models.

Somewhere along the way, the factory started using a foam core from about the waterline up. There are some weight savings on these later models, but of course they need to be examined carefully. In most cases, simply walking along all hori-

Years Produced	1978–2000
Designer	Roland and Francis Prout
Estimated Hulls Produced	600
Length Overall	37 feet
Length at Waterline	33 feet 4 inches
Draft (shoal/deep keel)	2 feet 8 inches
Beam	15 feet/16 feet Elite
Sail Area	660 square feet
Capsize Number	N/A
Displacement	11,000 lbs.
Ballast	N/A
Typical Engine	Volvo or Yanmar 30 hp
Fuel Capacity	18 gallons
Water Capacity	75 gallons
Typical Price Range	$40,000 USD and up
Owners Association(s)	www.michaelbriant.com

zontal surfaces will give you a quick idea if there are large problem areas.

The majority of these cats were built with one centerline diesel coupled to a retractable propulsion leg made by Sillette. As long as these units are never left too long in the down position, and are flushed as required, they last a long time. For those that need repairs, the company is still available since the largest multihull manufacturer in the United States—Gemini Corporation—is using these units. A few boats were made with twin diesels installed, allowing for the great maneuverability that twin-engine cats are famous for, but the Sonic leg works even if somewhat lacking in horsepower.

Describing the interior of any boat with words on paper is always a stretch, but in the case of a 40-year-old catamaran design, it is imperative to see for yourself. I know some would-be cruisers who decide on their dream boat without even seeing one, figuring they will like it based on reputation and research. Don't do that with a boat like the Snowgoose, especially if you have chartered a 40-footer in the Britsh Virgins or wherever. The boat is small for a catamaran, it is not much for light air, and typically you will either love it or hate it. In fact, Snowgoose owners remind me of Westsail 32 owners—defensive and ready to pounce.

If you have a family of four, the layout

Like many multihulls, the Snowgoose 37 can ease into shallow water. Having mini-keels protecting the rudders and running gear, this design can even be beached in calm conditions. Note the unusual cutter rig. (Courtesy Pete Hoggins)

of this boat is easily the best on The List for keeping everyone happy while living aboard. There are three separate bunks, and while they are not the queen-sized berths typical of Caribbean charter cats, they are big enough to let each family member have some space to themselves. This coupled with the essentially level sailing of multihulls makes for a family-friendly cruiser.

Entire books have been written about the pros and cons of multihulls and monohulls, so I won't try to review everything here. But I have done about 5,000 miles in multihulls and would offer these quick points.

A conservatively designed catamaran like the Prout Snowgoose has a minimal risk of capsize if cruising in season along the typical trade winds routes. These passages are of course downwind and the best point of sail for multihulls. If I was going to commute to work every day around Cape Horn, I would opt for a 60-foot aluminum monohull with watertight compartments, but for lower latitudes the Snowgoose has a great record.

As someone who started with multihulls but recently has owned monohulls, my switch was due to no longer doing much long-range cruising, and preferring a boat that could get into a California marina. You can get a lot of bang for your monohull buck right now, but it is worth noting that the Snowgoose can fit into a typical 45-foot marina slip. If I were going to resume serious cruising and anchor out a lot in tropical lagoons, I might see if I could afford a multihull, though it would be more of a preference than a requirement.

The Good, the Bad, and the Ugly

For tropical coral reef cruising, there is not much difference between a monohull with 6 feet of draft or one with 5 feet of draft. But the Snowgoose needs less than 3 feet of water and is designed to be beachable. There are cases of these boats getting caught in the surf at a Pacific island barrier reef and bouncing across and into the lagoon with hulls and rudders damaged but still serviceable. You can also sneak these boats deep into the mangroves as a hurricane berth. And once beached you will be level, resting on the minikeels.

Under sail, based on my experience there is no question that the Snowgoose would have a tough time tacking through better than 110 degrees on the open ocean. With her low bridgedeck clearance, she will also be noisy with some slamming when going to weather in rough seas. For those times when you need to furl the jib, trim the main in flat, and motorsail to weather into a 3-foot chop, a monohull is superior.

If windward performance is not a big factor in your cruising plans, these boats are strong, safe, and comfortable running before even brisk trade wind conditions. There is a reason why so many have circled the globe. So if you want an accessibly priced catamaran, the Snowgoose deserves a look.

With a production run of almost 400 boats, the Tartan 37—this one is Ron Marshall's Hobo— was one of the most popular U.S.-built cruiser-racers. Note the wide side decks and substantial gunwale for safety moving forward. (Courtesy Dick Dixon)

Tartan 37

Tartan Yachts founder Charlie Britton supposedly had his eyes set on racing when he commissioned the Tartan 37 design from Sparkman and Stephens. But although the hull showed a nice turn of speed, the boat would ultimately be more successful as a cruiser and demonstrates an excellent quality of construction and finish.

Tartan is one of a very few North American sailboat manufacturers that has remained in business continuously since the era of fiberglass boatbuilding began. It is still possible to order parts from the Ohio factory, and with a strong owners association a buyer of a 30-year-old example need not feel completely alone. With a production run of nearly 500 hulls (the majority being centerboard models), clearly they were doing something right with the 37.

I especially like the wide side decks and reasonably high bulwark on the 37, making for safer offshore work. But as this is a balsa-cored boat (both hull and deck), it is extremely important to have a good survey done prior to taking the plunge. Just as with C & C designs, there is nothing wrong with a balsa-cored boat provided the core has not been compromised. In a boat that may be 30 years old, you will have to be especially careful, and a bit lucky, to find an example that is completely intact. If the seller or another previous owner went a little overboard with deck fittings or solar panel mounts that were not properly bedded and installed, the deck core may have suffered from water intrusion and rot.

The cockpit is nicely sized, with a commodious lazarette and locker. The rudderpost has the usual emergency tiller access of aft cockpit boats, and below the waterline the rudder itself is supported by a skeg. Down below, the boat has a classic interior. There is a pilot berth above the starboard settee; these are rarely seen anymore, and in my experience are rarely used for sleeping. But if nothing else, the berth can work for light stowage such as bags of sails or clothing. Some owners have even done carpentry work and permanently converted the berth into cabinet stowage.

One of the best things about the T37 is that it came with a factory diesel, in all production years, that was adequate to push the boat. The Westerbeke 50 and 40 were the most common option, but the ubiquitous Perkins 4-108 was also used. Parts are still available for all these units, and the factory tankage of 50 gallons—while not overwhelming—is still better than that on most 37-footers and can be augmented if desired.

These are good sailors. Not surprisingly, the deep-draft version was reported to point a bit higher. The boat was not built to wrap itself around the IOR or any other ratings rule, so it tends to do all things well and is not excessively tender despite a rig that is tall enough to do well in light airs. East Coast sailors frequenting

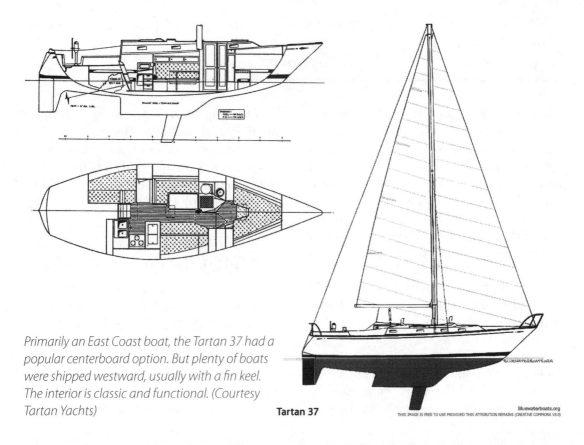

Primarily an East Coast boat, the Tartan 37 had a popular centerboard option. But plenty of boats were shipped westward, usually with a fin keel. The interior is classic and functional. (Courtesy Tartan Yachts)

Tartan 37

Bluewaterboats.org
THIS IMAGE IS FREE TO USE PROVIDED THIS ATTRIBUTION REMAINS (CREATIVE COMMONS V3.0)

Years Produced	1976–1988
Designer	Sparkman and Stephens
Estimated Hulls Produced	486
Length Overall	37 feet 3 inches
Length at Waterline	31 feet 7 inches
Draft (shoal/deep keel)	4 feet 2 inches/6 feet 7 inches
Beam	11 feet 9 inches
Sail Area	650 square feet
Capsize Number	1.8
Sail Area/Displacement Ratio	17
Displacement/Length Ratio	220
Displacement	15,500 lbs.
Ballast	7,500 lbs.
Mast Height Above Water	55 feet
Typical Engine	Westerbeke 40 or 50 hp
Fuel Capacity	50 gallons
Water Capacity	90 gallons
Typical Price Range	$35,000–$50,000 USD
Owners Association(s)	www.tartan37.com

Chesapeake Bay, the ICW, or the Bahamas will certainly opt for the centerboard, and they report no problems with centerboard operation or failure. On the West Coast, I really don't see much reason to take the centerboard over a standard keel.

Among the T37 circumnavigators, one of the better known was a ten-month voyage by Charl de Villiers. Deaf from age seven and a naturalized U.S. citizen by way of South Africa, Charl left from his home port of Palacios, Texas, and had a relatively trouble-free journey.

Norm and Lois Anderson did a leisurely circumnavigation from 1986 to 1993 aboard *Sisu*, and more recently *Tigger* went around. Its co-captain, Sharon Ragle, wrote a nice book about the trip

entitled *The Oceans Are Waiting: Around the World on the Yacht* Tigger.

Rouser was sailed by the Siegels from the West Coast to New Zealand, and as of this writing their blog is still available: http:/www.ourdotcom.com/family/Sailing_Adventures.html

The Good, the Bad, and the Ugly

This is a proven design with multiple circumnavigators within the owner ranks. The construction quality is very good. The fin keel model is harder to find, but the centerboard version has also proven its bluewater capability. The 37 has a simple rig and sail plan and is headsail driven. All owners report that the boat is a joy to sail.

It has a typical interior layout for this size, and the standard diesel was big enough to easily push the hull at 6 knots or better.

One problem that this design has seen over the years is a lower rudder pintle issue. It's not a fun thing to remedy, but there is excellent online assistance available via the owners organization website (www.tartan37.com). Tom Wells is the association's president and has been diligent in posting great technical articles at the site, covering various refinements.

"The decks are balsa cored with plywood in critical areas—foredeck and around the chainplates for two. The coring around the chainplates is subject to water entry. Many owners including me have made improvements here to seal the core off from the chainplate penetrations.

Also, there really is no bridgedeck, and the cockpit drains are a bit undersized. Some who've gone around have enlarged the drains. Some owners have also added a bridgedeck that doubles as storage for the life raft."

Finally, many of these boats came with a dark-colored factory gelcoat, especially black. This is certainly elegant, and for the northern climes works fine. But given that most cruising is done in the tropics, it is worth noting that a black or blue hull absorbs substantially more solar heat than a white one does, so the temperature in the cabin will be higher. This might call for an LP (linear polyurethane) paint job in the event you otherwise love your black-hulled Tartan 37 but intend to head for points south.

Sagacious sports the darker hull color of many original Tartan 37s. Note how well the Sparkman and Stephens–designed hull moves in light conditions under a chute. (Courtesy Peter Haeni and Tom Wells)

The hugely popular Tayana 37 was the breakthrough design of Robert Perry. It combines a traditional teak-laden exterior with a cutaway full keel that made her a respectable performer. (Courtesy Janice Nagle at www.sailacious.com)

Tayana 37

In the mid-1970s a founder of Flying Dutchman Yachts in Seattle, Bob Berg, was amazed to see how much of a success the Westsail 32 had been in the market. The boat had made the cover of *Time* magazine and was at the forefront of a new counterculture movement for those wanting to drop out of the rat race and head for warm waters. Boats were being built in backyards by hippies who had scraped up enough to buy a hull and others with more cash who bought factory-finished versions. Slickly produced glossy ads showed them how one could chuck the trappings of modern life and live off the sea. Cruising went as mainstream as it ever would.

Berg and partner Will Eckert decided to try to improve on the concept and commissioned a young Northwest yacht designer named Robert Perry to draw a longer boat with the similar classic Colin Archer canoe stern and plenty of teak, capped off with a salty bowsprit.

The group then approached Taiwanese builder Ta Chiao (builders of the prolific CT series), and one or two boats were made as the CT 37 before the yard decided to drop out, apparently thinking the boat would not be a winner. In what was the yachting equivalent of Wally Pipp giving up first base to Lou Gehrig, the Ta-Yang yard agreed to build the design, and the Tayana 37 was born. The first few were built by Ta-Yang but labeled CT37s, until the Tayana name took over on what was an identical boat.

Suffice it to say that after more than 600 hulls and counting, the Tayana 37 has been the most successful cruising boat ever built. According to the Tayana Owners Group, the words Ta Yang mean "Big Ocean," and if you substitute an *a* for the *g* at the end, the word Tayana means "Belongs to the Big Ocean." Considering that probably dozens of T37s have circumnavigated, it is certainly appropriate. At anchor, it is hard to head for shore in your dinghy and not look back admiringly at a boat that looks the epitome of a bluewater cruiser.

Although I am not a big fan of full-keel boats even for cruising, this design is no slouch once the wind gets above 10 knots. I have sailed several T37s and, properly trimmed, they can clip along quite well. The keel is not quite truly full, with a nicely tapered entry at the forefoot. The chord, or width, is not excessive, so this may help its hydrodynamics. I also contacted legendary designer Robert Perry and he confirmed that paying special attention to the T37 keel was paramount:

"The trick with all my early double-enders was to treat the keel and the canoe body as separate entities. So when it came to the keel design, I just applied the same theory that I used for fin keel boats. Of course I had to modify the foils for that long, full keel. And, I must say that looking back I could have done an even better job than I did."

Years Produced	1976–present
Designer	Robert Perry
Estimated Hulls Produced	700
Length Overall	36 feet 9 inches
Length at Waterline	31 feet
Draft	5 feet 8 inches
Beam	11 feet 6 inches
Sail Area	841 square feet (cutter)
Capsize Number	1.6
Sail Area/Displacement Ratio	17
Displacement/Length Ratio	337
Displacement	22,500 lbs.
Ballast	7,340 lbs.
Typical Engine	Volvo or Yanmar 3-cylinder
Fuel Capacity	90 gallons
Water Capacity	110 gallons
Typical Price Range	$30,000–$95,000 USD
Owners Association(s)	http://www.tognews.com

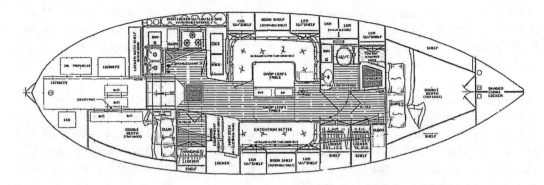

As a semi-custom boat, the Tayana 37 had a number of variations to the interior. Shown is the most popular version on a hull that was produced for well over twenty years.

Perry may feel he could have gone even further, but if you have been to Taiwan factories as I have, or even just seen these Taiwanese keels in U.S. boatyards over the years, you know that keels from that era were not sleek bolt-on NACA foils but fat, drag-inducing wedges that were used to encapsulate whatever scrap iron or lead was available. The Tayana keel was an evolution significantly above those.

But the devil is in the details, so let's look at some of the finer points of a very popular design, although it had many incarnations.

For one thing, the boat was offered as a cutter or a ketch, or even with a pilothouse. Since the interior could be customized to the buyer's tastes, the only truly consistent aspect to the boat throughout the almost forty years of building is the hull itself. But what a hull it is. Carrying the beam well aft makes for a generous interior, but thankfully Perry did not copy the Westsail 32's overkill in the beam department. With her canoe stern, she leaves a clean wake even heeled, and the T37 goes to weather quite well with a cutter rig.

Numerous engine options were seen over the decades, and the factory encour-

aged owner participation on the interior. But the most common models had the ubiquitous quarter berth aft and V-berth forward (shown in this chapter). It is hard to say which engine was the most popular, but the earliest hull numbers seemed to have Volvos, and then more Yanmars came along. Note that most of the Tayanas that I found below $50,000 were pre-1985 and had as many Volvo Pentas as Yanmars.

Although the hull is solid glass, the decks were/are balsa cored and can have issues. Given that there can be hundreds of screws drilled into the deck to fasten the teak planking, you will want to check as carefully as possible. With a potential purchase, I always like to spray the deck with a hose for a good 15 minutes to check for leaks, but your broker or seller may not allow this.

The water tanks were usually made of black iron and often rusted to the point of needing replacement. A new polyethylene tank is cheap enough as long as you don't have to take a chainsaw to the boat to get the old one out and the new one in. As a rule, if you are buying a boat from the 1970s that has had no upgrades, you will need to check everything. Be especially cautious with the rigging, the decks and deck fittings, and tank condition. The earliest boats had spruce spars, so add this to your maintenance calendar if you like to stay busy, or keep looking for a boat with an aluminum mast.

These boats have a following, so be prepared to put in some sweat equity on any boats available for under the $50,000 threshold. A typical story is a boat purchased with bluewater cruising in mind and then has sat for years at a dock while time and the sun ate away at the teak and the canvas. Hopefully the interior is intact, and you will just have to decide if bringing the exterior back and/or removing the teak decks will be worth it to you. Much will depend on the included equipment. If you want a windvane, there are more windvane-equipped T37s available than any other design treated here.

Although there were some ketch and pilothouse models ordered, the majority of the Tayana 37s were cutter rigged. It is hard to deny the great flexibility offered by this sail plan, especially going to weather. In my experience sailing her it was no problem to roll up the Yankee and continue to weather in 35 knots with a staysail and reefed main. Some owners have complained about excessive weather helm, but the boat I was delivering appeared to have the mast raked forward somewhat. With proper traveler use, weather helm was typical. Downwind, of course, the advantages of a cutter rig are somewhat diminished.

Interior plans are hard to treat here since there were so many variations. You will have to look at each layout individually, but if you're searching on YachtWorld there should be enough photos to help give you an initial impression. But no matter what, the interior teak will be everywhere.

Remember that an amateur with a varnish brush (or palm sander) can easily ruin the appearance and value of what was a gorgeous interior. So hopefully yours has not been compromised, and if it needs work you will ensure that you are not a danger to her due to a lack of experience. It is worth noting that the cruisers I met who loved their Tayanas (or other Taiwan Teakies) were all excellent at sanding and varnishing and that it was usually the female who was better at it.

Here's one other comment about teaky interiors that is often overlooked. They do not like to be left unattended in the tropics. Many cruisers are now commuting back and forth between their boats and the real world, so if you think you can leave your boat for months at a time in a humid environment and return to step aboard and go, think again. Since the tropics mean rain, you will doubtless have the boat locked up while you are gone, and the amount of mold that can build up in six months is impressive. Cabinet doors may not close, and exterior varnish may be peeling. Of course this is without considering what may happen to the canvas or the engine.

What is it they say? "Cruising is yacht maintenance in exotic ports."

The Good, the Bad, and the Ugly

If you like a truly salty and traditional look, then here is your boat. They have proven seakeeping abilities and a great following that keep their resale value quite a bit higher than comparable Taiwanese boats of this size. The rare pilothouse model will not be available for under $50,000, but it has nice lines on what is often an awkward design challenge for boats under 40 feet. The T37 also has a great owners association, which can come in handy when you are trying to figure out the best windvane steering unit for that canoe stern.

Unless the decks have been replaced, you will get to spend plenty of time keeping the teak in order. For some sailors, this is a labor of love they actually enjoy, but for others it gets pretty old after about the third coat of varnish on the glossy areas. Don't forget the kneepads.

Other than the high maintenance, the Ugly would have to include the difficulty of mounting a below-decks autopilot on Tayanas that have worm-gear steering. A worm-gear system is extremely strong but does not lend itself to a ram-type autopilot, so bear this in mind if you don't enjoy steering by hand. Even if you have a windvane, an autopilot is very nice for mo-

torsailing. Fortunately the later T37s had conventional cable and sheave steering.

Owner Comments

"We love our boat, but it is not for everyone. It is a very capable cruising boat for two as it is very forgiving and has large tankage for extended periods away from services. We will weigh the anchor and go when others will wait for a better (perfect) weather window. The boat is built like a tank and weighs as much. We put in a new through-hull about 6 inches above the waterline for the watermaker discharge and found that the fiberglass was ⅝ inch thick!"

—Janice Nagle, co-owner
Sailacious

Sailacious *on a mooring at Warderick Wells, Exuma Cays Land and Sea Park, Bahamas. At the time the Tayana 37 came along, the preference amongst most bluewater aspirants was a solid fiberglass hull, heavy layup, cutter rig, and no more than 40 feet to be easily handled by a couple. (Courtesy Janice Nagle)*

Bagheera is just one of several Beneteau 38s that have circumnavigated, in this case with a family of four aboard. Her sleek lines and solid build make the design just as attractive today as when it was launched over thirty years ago. (Courtesy Liza Copeland)

Beneteau First 38

The Beneteau 38 offers such sleek and stylish lines that one may not see it as a potential globe-girdling cruiser. But according to Liza and Andy Copeland, no fewer than five Beneteau First 38s have circumnavigated. They should know since they were one of them, having gone around from 1985 to 1991 on *Bagheera* with three sons aboard. Andy was actually a Beneteau dealer, and they obtained their boat new from France in an era when (even as today) many experts were insisting that a moderate-displacement fin keel boat was not appropriate for bluewater passagemaking. Other than some upgrades to the rigging, she was a stock boat, though it was fully outfitted right down to the windvane on the transom.

Some 80,000 miles later, there are no better experts on this design than the Copelands. "The Beneteau First 38s is a Jean Beret–designed sloop introduced into the European market in 1979 with both medium- and deep-draft versions available. A tall double-spreader "S" rig—keel-stepped as opposed to the standard deck-stepped single-spreader rig—was available also. In 1985, the tooling was updated to become the First 405 using the same hull and keel but with a modified deck and interior."

I have only a few days' sailing time on this design,

but in Ventura, California, I went out on a friend's Beneteau one windy afternoon, and the performance of his 38 did not disappoint. We tacked easily through 90 degrees and sometimes higher, with a well-balanced helm in over 20 knots of breeze near the Channel Islands. At one point we were sailing hard into a 3-foot chop—something that unfortunately many cruisers can relate to—and although I was worried that her bow entry might be too flat and result in pounding, the boat behaved nicely. Later when we were able to crack off on a broad reach, the owner commented that the boat could occasionally surf on long waves.

I took some time on the day sail to check below. Beneteau used a grid liner system fiberglassed into the bilge, as well as standard glasswork to ensure proper tabbing between the bulkheads and the hull. This made for a rigid yet not overly heavy build. I was impressed with the lack of flexing or leaks below, even when pounding hard to weather. This was something backed up by Liza Copeland in my later communications with her as well as her own reviews on the boat. She mentions that the First 38 earned the highest rating possible for "unlimited offshore use" under the strict French federal certification program.

It was also amazing how much had been fit into a 38-foot hull, including two quarter cabins as a nod to the boat's intended use for the Caribbean charter market. The aft head is tucked in between these cabins, a bit oddly located behind

Years Produced	1982–1986
Designer	Jean Beret
Estimated Hulls Produced	403
Length Overall	38 feet 6 inches
Length at Waterline	33 feet 8 inches
Draft	6 feet 10 inches
Beam	12 feet 10 inches
Sail Area	850 square feet
Capsize Number	2.0
Sail Area/Displacement Ratio	21.7
Displacement/Length Ratio	183
Displacement	15,655 lbs.
Ballast	6,615 lbs.
Mast Height Above Water	50 feet
Typical Engine	Perkins 50 hp
Fuel Capacity	44 gallons
Water Capacity	100 gallons
Typical Price Range	$35,000–$50,000 USD
Owners Association(s)	www.beneteau.sailboatowners.com

*The Beneteau 38—*Arcadia *shown here—is just as at home on the race course as she is crossing oceans. (Courtesy owner James Jelsone)*

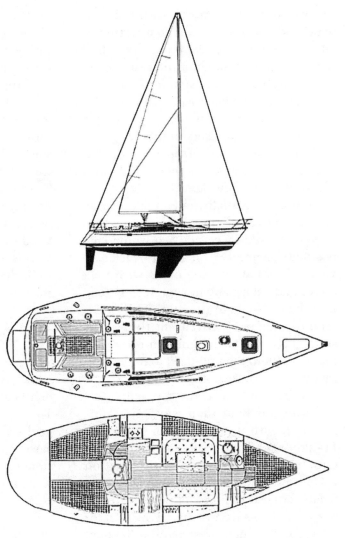

Perhaps with the Caribbean bareboat trade in mind, the Beneteau First 38 managed to squeeze two private quarter cabins under the cockpit. If you have kids cruising with you, the quarter cabins will be handy; otherwise, they may become seagoing garages. (Courtesy Beneteau USA)

and under the companionway. The Copelands relegated this to storage use, but you could also turn the V-berth over to stowage and still have two decent berths aft, where the motion at sea is more comfortable. Cockpit lockers are, of course, compromised whenever the area underneath is devoted to sleeping quarters.

What is most impressive, however, is the huge dinette, which designer Jean Beret decided to place at the boat's maximum beam. With a centerline table and the set-

tee to starboard, you can actually seat six or more comfortably, an incredible feat for a 38-footer. And while the look of the Beneteau exterior is all low-maintenance white fiberglass, down below there is a generous use of teak, which makes for a yachty feel. There are gracefully curved fiddles and nicely varnished surfaces everywhere.

As with most French designs, there are very few 90 degree angles. All the doors are curved, and the teak has a darker tone than that on American boats. Overall this works well in contrast with the light overhead liners and head compartment, although some potential buyers may find that they prefer a brighter interior.

These boats came standard with the Perkins 4-108, which is a pleasant surprise on a size of boat that typically gets only a 30 horsepower specified on the designer's desk. With nearly 50 horsepower, the Perkins can easily push the boat, and parts are available worldwide.

A few 38s actually had a teak overlay on the decks as an option, but one would have to question whether that would be a positive or a negative on a boat nearing 30 years old. I have owned boats with teak above and below, and now prefer my teak only below—out of the sun! The Beneteau deck is balsa cored but the hull is solid glass, and the aluminum toe rail is integrated into the hull-deck joint, as with many racer-cruisers of that era.

There is a less secure feel going forward on this boat than, say, on a Morgan 382, with its nice 5-inch gunwales. Frankly my advice to my instruction clients has always been to put the boat on its feet by luffing up for a moment to do whatever needs doing, so that crew-member safety is ensured. Stopping the boat for 30 seconds to clear a snag on a jibsheet is hardly a consequential delay if you are on a two-week crossing to the Marquesas. But having said this, racer-cruisers like the Beneteau, the Newport, the Catalina, and the C & C are slightly more dangerous in terms of the potential for slipping when moving forward.

The quality of the rig stands out, and I am a big fan of anodized aluminum masts such as the French-made Isomat that came on some of these boats. An anodized mast has much less maintenance than a

painted one, and is always preferable. The shrouds are placed so that proper sheeting angles can always be obtained, and the chainplates transfer their loads properly to structural members below.

Although the First 38 may not conform with what some cruisers are looking for in terms of bowsprits, long keels, and skeg rudders, in the really important ways this boat is as ruggedly built as any heavy Taiwan Teakie out there. With at least five having circumnavigated, the boat has credentials beyond reproach, and they are readily available under $50,000. If you are a cruiser who actually likes to sail and sail well, the First 38 should be on your very short list.

The Good, the Bad, and the Ugly

The good is that somehow this design packs three private sleeping compartments and two heads into a 38-foot boat. The bad, well, is that this design somehow packs all this into a 38-foot boat. In the case of the Copeland's *Bagheera*, for instance, they ended up using the aft head for more stowage. Cockpit locker stowage is also reduced due to the quarter cabins. It is a completely different approach than, say, the Golden Wave 42 or the CSY 37 B Plan, which are optimized for one couple. What I like most about this boat is the construction quality, low maintenance, great sailing performance, and berthing options for a family.

There were some blister issues in the 1980s, but Beneteau paid for these repairs, and virtually all the First Series should be blister free. One significant issue on some of the Beneteaus of this era is adhesion failure on the overhead liner. Droopy liner syndrome (DLS) may seem like a pretty minor issue, but it is a fairly difficult job if the problem has advanced to the point where the entire vinyl liner has to be pulled and either reattached or replaced.

Commentary from
Circumnavigator Liza Copeland

"Besides its performance, workable deck design, and comfortable cockpit, we were attracted to the layout below. For our family of five, the accommodation works well: two aft double cabins, workable galley, large chart table with abundant space for electronics, long settee/sea berths, full-sized table in the main cabin, and spacious forward cabin.

Bagheera is a dry boat, thanks to its moderate displacement and reserve buoyancy in the ends. We love the finger-light steering in all conditions, a sail plan that can be handled by a single not-so-young watchkeeper, and the performance that has allowed us to average more than 150 miles per day on all our ocean crossings. To us, she is the perfect combination of seakindliness, seaworthiness, and fun on the ocean, and she's a comfortable home at anchor to boot."

It's hard to improve on the original brochure shot of a 1981 Ericson 38. Like all Bruce King designs, the 38 had sweet lines that made her a popular racer.

Ericson 38

The original Ericson 38 began production in 1979 and went through several evolutions—primarily in the interior layout—until Pacific Seacraft bought the company and came out with the 380. The 380 is a great boat but rarely seen for under $50,000, so it will be the original 1980s versions that are treated here. This is hardly a downgrade since there may not be a designer better than Bruce King for drawing sweet-sailing yachts with a timeless sheer. These boats had a couple of new designations as they evolved through the 1980s and are usually referred to as the 38 (1980), the 381 (1983), and then the 38-200 (from 1986 until 1990). The last Ericson-built version, the 38-200, is difficult but not impossible to find within a $50,000 budget.

Some of my earliest sailing experiences were on San Francisco Bay aboard Bruce King designs like the 32, 35, and 38. Bruce did not like slow boats, and you could see the inclination toward performance in his double-spreader rigs, inboard shrouds for tighter sheeting angles, and a minimal use of wood or sheathing, which added to the weight. All three designs had a T-cockpit and what for the time was a huge wheel on a racer-cruiser, but the traveler bridging the cockpit on the smaller boats was thankfully

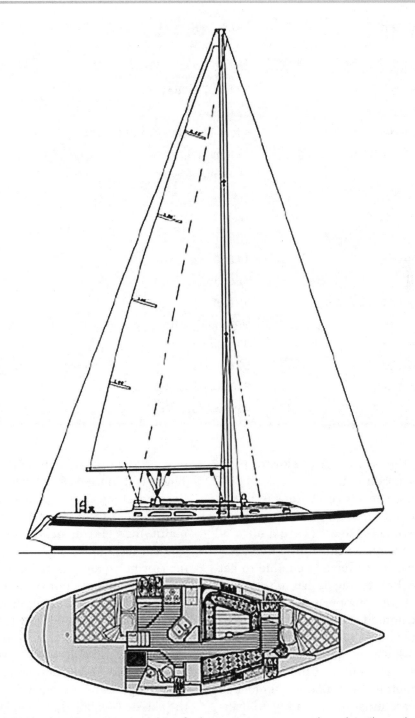

The Ericson 38-200 had a private quarter cabin aft plus a mini-settee to starboard similar to that on the Catalina 36. After Pacific Seacraft bought the Ericson molds, a final version, the Ericson 380, came out with yet another interior.

Years Produced	1979–1990
Designer	Bruce King
Estimated Hulls Produced	200
Length Overall	37 feet 7 inches
Length at Waterline	32 feet
Draft (shoal/deep keel)	4 feet 11 inches/6 feet 6 inches
Beam	12 feet
Sail Area	709 square feet
Capsize Number	1.8
Sail Area/Displacement Ratio	18.8
Displacement/Length Ratio	202
Displacement	14,850 lbs.
Ballast	6,300 lbs.
Mast Height Above Water	55 feet
Typical Engine	Universal 32 hp
Fuel Capacity	59 gallons
Water Capacity	60 gallons
Typical Price Range	$38,000–$60,000 USD
Owners Association	www.ericsonyachts.org

moved on the 38 to a less awkward position on the coachroof.

Keeping the traveler accessible is somewhat important on the 38 because in my experience these boats are a bit tender. They balance beautifully, however, and in most seas I have been able to get almost any Bruce King design to self-steer to weather for long periods once it was properly trimmed. This was the first boat I can remember where I could really understand what it meant to be sailing "in the groove." The entry at the bow is fine enough to minimize pounding—in fact so fine that care must be taken not to overload the bow area with two anchors, excess chain, etc.

Down below, the look is the complete opposite of, for instance, the Tayana 37. There is a limited use of teak on the earliest versions, but it makes for a more open feel, and most surfaces are easily maintained via an occasional wipe down. The earliest models had a non-partitioned quarter berth aft to port, while later boats had some sort of door or divider used to separate the quarter cabin from the main saloon. My personal favorite is the 38-200, which has a fully enclosed quarter cabin for privacy and a decent shower arrangement in the head compartment. There also seems to be a nicer use of teak, and the classic U-galley is as refined as you can ask for.

Ericson was an early believer in bonding floor molds, bulkheads, and stress areas together with the hull for stiffness and strength. In fact it was noted racing designer Dave Pedrick who laid out what Ericson called the "triaxial grid" to tie in all the major load points. There are conspicuous tie rods for the shrouds that terminate in aluminum blocks cast into structural members port and starboard, a product of having the shrouds well inboard. The hull is solid glass, but coring was used on most of the deck and needs to be checked carefully on what could be a 30-year-old boat. Some core was balsa, and most areas taking winches and fittings were plywood cored.

The hull-to-deck joint was essentially a glass-to-glass joint with no dependency on fasteners. The side decks are wide and easily negotiated, somewhat more friendly than, say, the Islander 36 or Newport 41 but not as safe as the Morgan 382 or a Tayana. Although the inboard shrouds are partly to blame for this, these Ericsons are headsail-driven boats and can point higher than any boat in this book with the jib or genny trimmed in tight to less than 10 degrees. Tacking angles can easily be under 90 degrees in moderate sea and wind conditions.

The Good, the Bad, and the Ugly

There were enough of these built that at any given time there should be at least a few on the market below $50,000 with good equipment lists, primarily the original model. All versions are dynamite sailors but especially those with the deep or "competition" keel option. In my experience, Ericsons are initially tender but then

The Ericson 38 Southern Cross *about to leave Los Cabos, Mexico, for a successful crossing to the Marquesas Islands. Skipper Mark Reed supervises Vicki Bugbee-Reed with the romantic task of laundering while cruising.*

Ericson 38 Cappuccino *racing on San Francisco Bay. (Courtesy Kevin Murray)*

stabilize nicely after perhaps 20 degrees of heel. Stiffness may increase once the boat is loaded for cruising.

I am not a big fan of hatchboards and prefer companionways small and square enough to accept small, stout doors if they are not already fitted. Fortunately the Ericson does not have the usual big trapezoid companionway entrance typical of the era, and my first project would be to junk the hatchboards in favor of small doors on good knuckle hinges. As to other projects, some owners have found the standard bow

locker inadequate and have made modifications accordingly.

The oldest boats sometimes showed significant blistering and could leak via deck fittings and ports once the sealants aged enough. Deck leaks rarely show up in a survey, but there is often staining on interior surfaces that will give it away. Or if possible, check to see if the seller or broker will let you turn a hose on the decks and ports for a few minutes, and then check below.

Owner Comments

"I race Alliance on Wednesdays and in weekend regattas so the wing keel is not doing me any favors. The keel had leaked, but I had it dropped and resealed. The 5'5" draft is nice, but I do not want the wing keel stuck in the mud! I love the overall construction of the hull, the way the deck is bonded with the boat, and the protected chainplates. She handles well, turns on a dime, and is easy to park for a 38' boat. I love the look of the very roomy interior, but, when cruising, there's little space for storage. I tried to install an air conditioning unit but gave up due to the lack of space. I like the contours of the cockpit—roomy with no sharp corners. I have all lines running aft so singlehanding is a breeze. I wish there was more room to install additional winches for flying a spinnaker. Overall I am in love with the boat and I am very happy I purchased Alliance."

—Mark Stetler, owner Ericson 38-2,
Alliance

With over 200 boats built, the Hans Christian 38 can be found in cruising crossroads around the world. This is *Horizon* anchored off Moorea in the South Pacific. (Courtesy Marci Paravia)

Hans Christian 38

By now you have had time to review the boats I have included on The List, and it should be clear that I am not a big fan of heavy, full-keel crab crushers. I have delivered over twenty, and while they can give you a Cadillac ride when sailing into a chop in a stiff breeze, if you like to sail in lighter winds, you may find yourself frustrated. The Tayana 37, for instance—with a much more hydrodynamic cutaway keel than on the HC 38—is, in my opinion, a better-sailing boat. But given that most of one's time cruising is spent at anchor and not under way, the difference between completing a passage in seven days versus eight days is not always that significant.

So although my inclusion of the Hans Christian 38 will have some caveats, I felt that, with a substantial production run of around 220 hulls, a standard Yanmar diesel, excellent tank capacity, and passable quality of build, the boat merited attention. Just because I probably would not choose it as my own cruiser does not mean that you shouldn't. She does have beautiful lines and a nice interior, and was typically cutter rigged, so there is a lot to be said for her. And they can be had for $50,000 or less. My own YachtWorld search turned up two at or below $50,000 and two others around $60,000 as an asking price.

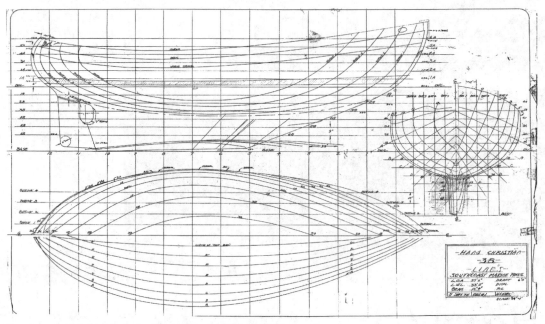

The standard full keel used on the majority of the HC 38s.

These boats came in a lot of semi-custom configurations, and luckily the strong owners association (www.hanschristian. org) can provide details and feedback far beyond what I have space for here. Instead I think it is more informative to look in depth at the most important shift in boatbuilding and boat marketing that the industry has seen other than the invention of fiberglass. By this I mean the shift in the 1970s and 1980s from United States production to the Far East, notably Taiwan and Hong Kong. And there is no better example of that phenomenon than Hans Christian Yachts.

The entire Hans Christian story is an interesting mix of personalities. The actual designer of the 38, Harwood "Woody" Ives, was in Taiwan building a ferro-cement boat for himself when company founder John Edwards came across him and was impressed by his natural design ability. Neither Edwards (originally a school-teacher) nor Ives had any formal training as naval architects, but Edwards had had a falling out with Robert Perry, who had designed the HC 34, and he hired Woody Ives on the spot. The HC 36 had been literally a stretched version of the 34, but the 38 was an Ives design that did not "borrow" (to put it politely) from Perry. Of course both Perry and Ives borrowed heavily from Colin Archer in using the traditional full keel and canoe stern on the original HC 38. They also continued an effort by many builders at the time to duplicate the success of the Westsail 32, but with a more inspiring performance.

In researching this chapter, I came across other reviews and websites that had a lot of conflicting information on the total production run and versions of the HC 38. Until about 1983, they were all built at the Shin Fa yard, then later they were built primarily in Thailand. So I was happy to reach the person who probably knows more about the design than any other—Craig Beckwith. He was the vice president of sales for Hans Christian over almost its entire history, and when I spoke with him he was able to clarify what happened over the years with the 38:

"There were no more than 130 built of the Traditional, and the last 30 had the Telstar keel. The first version with the traditional full keel had pretty severe weather helm, so only a couple of years after we started building them, the Mark II was introduced with some hull improvements and the mast moved forward about a foot. She also had more sail area, but although the weather helm was reduced somewhat, the boat was still overpowered and we didn't really get it right until the Telstar keel was introduced."

Most of the HC 38s had a full keel that did not perform as well as the hybrid "Telstar" keel shown. The interiors were available in a number of semi-custom options. (Courtesy designer Woody Ives)

At this point the yard had the new HC 38 Mark II molds and also the original two HC 38 Traditional molds. Since the Mark II was an improvement but not a complete solution, in an effort to reduce the weather helm, company founder Edwards decided to take a gamble and experiment with one of the two molds from the original boat. Without any real calculations or drafting to back him up, he instructed the yard where he wanted to reduce the keel area into more of a tapered entry. He then made a drastic notch aft, resulting in a skeg rudder on a cutaway full keel.

Beckwith reports that everyone was on pins and needles when the first new boat was finished. "We were worried, but the Telstar keel was great. She tacked better, and the boat was faster and more buoyant and stiffer."

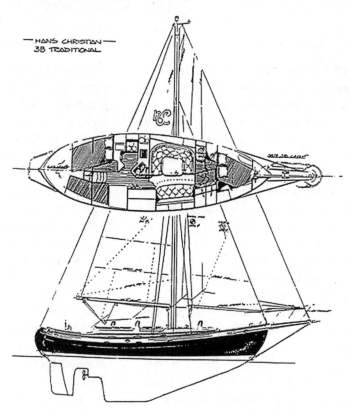

— HANS CHRISTIAN —
38 TRADITIONAL

Years Produced	1976–1989
Designer	Harwood Ives
Estimated Hulls Produced	136 Traditional/86 Mark II
Length On Deck	38 feet
Length at Waterline	33 feet
Draft (shoal/deep keel)	6 feet
Beam	12 feet 4 inches
Sail Area	791 square feet
Capsize Number	1.6
Sail Area/Displacement Ratio	14.2
Displacement/Length Ratio	329
Displacement	26,500 lbs.
Ballast	9,800 lbs.
Typical Engine	35 hp Yanmar
Fuel Capacity	100 gallons
Water Capacity	100 gallons
Typical Price Range	$50,000–$100,000 USD
Most Active Owners Association	www.hanschristian.org

The Telstar keel came on line in 1985, and about thirty were built until production of all HC versions stopped in 1989. Today the Telstar keel option is highly sought after and will rarely be seen in the $50,000 price range. But for budget cruisers, the Traditional or Mark II without the updated keel can still be a viable option. The sail area will need to be kept manageable and the mast perhaps raked forward, but many owners are happy with their choice once they know how to sail the boat. Reportedly more standard keels have circumnavigated than the sleeker cutaway.

Perhaps trying to match the custom interior options of the Tayana 37, the HC 38 had at least three interiors offered over its history. There was a "Pullman berth" option, a "V-berth option," and an unpopular "head forward" option. If anyone has

ever tried keeping stable or seated while up forward in a small sailboat going to weather, it is little wonder that the "head forward" version fizzled out.

I have flown on several occasions to Taiwan on behalf of owners having boats built there, usually large powerboats, and the quality of the product put out by Taiwan yards can vary tremendously. Otto Von Bismark once said that his citizens should never see what went in to the making of German law or German sausages. The same could be said of what goes in to the keel voids on Taiwanese sailboats. Since three different yards built the 38 over the years, not surprisingly the quality did vary, and when talking to Craig Beckwith I felt obliged to run a story by him to see his reaction.

In 2001 I was in La Paz, Mexico, when

Hurricane Juliette came through. Although the winds did not exceed 70 miles per hour, we received 34 inches of rain in three days. At a local storage facility that did not have a cement yard surface, the tremendous amount of water caused all the jack stands to start to sink into the ground, and once the boats starting leaning over they fell like dominos. In all, about twenty boats toppled, and I ended up doing casualty surveys on many of them. A few boats impacted down onto the jack stand as they fell, which in some cases caused a deep gouge. But in the case of a Hans Christian 36, the jack stand actually holed the boat at the turn of the bilge.

This was a little surprising to me, but when I looked closer I could see that, although there was almost ⅝ inch of fiberglass mat and roving in the laminate, the resin had not properly penetrated the glass, and I was able to grab the cloth and move it around easily due to it being dry. In other words, the factory had plenty of cloth present, but they had not properly "wetted out" the laminates beyond a quarter inch on the outside and slightly less than that inside.

When I told Craig Beckwith about this, to his credit he acknowledged that some of the HC hulls had indeed been subpar. "The 33 was the best built because we had a fastidious German guy watching over that production. But it's true there were some 34s, 36s, and 38s that did not get the same sort of supervision, and some of the hulls suffered from that with dry layup."

I was fortunate to reach Harwood "Woody" Ives, the actual HC 38 designer, and he also confirmed the quality of the 33 and the possible drop in quality of the later 38s, especially those built in Thailand:

"The 38 T was built only by Shin Fa to my knowledge. The 38 MK II was built at the Hai O by Tommy Chen, and the pilothouse version of that by another yard. We tried hard to inspect each hull every day through her production cycle, which was a difficult logistical challenge at times, especially during peak production, so there was some inconsistency. I'd venture that the early to mid years of production of the 38T were good. I had Hull 44. And I was not involved in the production, only design, after 1977. Long after I was gone, the production moved to Thailand, and I have no knowledge of that at all. The 33s, probably a couple hundred of them, were built by a highly talented German, Herb Guttler, at the Hansa yard. He physically built them himself. He had a lot of sea experience and knew what was required, so in a way his product was the most consistent and highest quality that Hans ever got while I was involved."

Since these boats are overbuilt to begin with, there is usually plenty of reserve strength as long as there are no point-loaded impacts. A wave hitting a boat does not have the localized impact of, say, the bow of a Mexican panga or a boatyard jack stand. So for me, to be clear, I would not hesitate to step aboard any of the 38s and head for Fatu Hiva. But if I hit a reef, I would not expect the boat to last any longer than an American production boat with a thinner laminate but (presumably) a properly laid up hull. Fiberglass cloth by itself has no strength; it needs to be properly wetted out.

There are so many variations on the interiors of these boats that I do not try to detail them here, other than to say that a very common layout managed to tuck both a double and a single berth aft under the cockpit. This sort of berth arrangement

Although the rudderstock carries all the way up the transom, most of the HC 38s actually had wheel steering. The wide teak side decks offer safe footing but can be a maintenance nightmare once they start leaking into the deck coring. (Courtesy Woody Ives)

makes for some comfortable sea berths on either tack, but the locker stowage in the cockpit of course suffers. The traditional U-galley was phased out in the Mark II version with an unusual "island sink" arrangement that prospective buyers seem to either love or hate.

In my two times sailing the H-38, both times the full-keel version, the weather helm was evident. But the owners had learned to adjust, in one case by raking the mast forward and in the other case always rolling up the Yankee once the wind went above 18 knots. Tracking downwind was a strong point—a frequent benefit of a full keel.

A few months before this book's publication, the story of a Hans Christian 36

made international news when it had to be abandoned about a thousand miles into a passage from Mexico to the Marquesas. *Rebel Heart* had a family of four aboard, including two infants, but although there was a structural issue, ultimately it was the deteriorating health of the one-year-old that caused the abandonment of the boat. *Latitude 38* (May 12, 2014) provided further details.

According to Eric Kaufman, on their fifteenth day out, the day before they called for help, they sailed into the Intertropical Convergence Zone (ITCZ) where they met with strong winds and big seas. Charlotte explains that they were knocked down several times. But one particular broach stressed the boat so much that it began leaking along the starboard hull-deck joint and elsewhere (unspecified). The resulting inflow of seawater was estimated at 60 to 70 gallons per day. Meanwhile, one-year-old Lyra had been ill since day seven. As Charlotte explains, the infant developed a widespread rash, had diarrhea, and became lethargic . . .

The couple discussed their options, with Eric calculating that it would be another three weeks before they would arrive in the Marquesas—if their pumping could keep up with the incoming water. "What would you do?" he asks rhetorically of his radio audience. As Charlotte explains, the decision was heartbreaking: "You know if you hit the EPIRB, help will come, but if you hit it, your home is gone."

So while the apparent failure of the hull-deck joint is serious and merits further investigation, it was not the sometimes poor layup of these (and other) boats that led to the abandonment. In fact, had the Coast Guard not discharged a few hundred rounds of lead into the hull to avoid leaving a navigation hazard, it would not have surprised me to learn that *Rebel Heart* was seen floating weeks later. The adults on board had to make an adult decision, and while many pundits thought their mistake had been leaving the docks of Puerta Vallarta with infants aboard to start with, I can say that I have seen dozens of yachts over the years cruising with young children aboard. Maybe only a handful with a one-year-old, but it has been done.

The Kaufmans lost their home and the only significant possession they had, but they kept their daughter. Would any other parent faced with the same situation have acted differently?

The Good, the Bad, and the Ugly

These boats are usually bought with blue-water in mind, so many are well equipped. A Yanmar was the typical diesel, and that is always a plus. Most have a dodger, but the canoe stern is a bit awkward for windvanes, so if you want one, try to find one with a unit already installed, even if it costs you an extra several thousand. Installing them from scratch is expensive.

Most had a 100-gallon fuel tank standard, best in The List. Cutter rigs are also very nice, and going forward on the wide side decks of the HC 38 is a safer proposition than on most boats. There is a very strong owners association, so if your boat came at a great price due to teak decks that need replacing, online support is available.

The majority of the boats had a full keel and developed plenty of weather helm with the bowsprit-mounted headstay. The light air performance of a 38-footer weighing as much as these designs is also never going to be a strong point. Due to the cutter rig and canoe stern, dinghy stowage is problematic. I have seen some with davits, but they look awful. Davits rarely make sense on boats under 44 feet, if then.

Ugly would certainly not describe this boat. She looks like the perfect cruiser no matter where she is anchored. But all that beautiful exterior teak comes with a price, so bring your kneepads for those days of sanding, and worship to Makita, the Japanese god of brightwork.

The Morgan 382 (Dana) achieves a rare consensus among the pundits as a great candidate for a well-built budget cruiser. Due to long overhangs, the waterline is only 30 feet, but a modern underbody helps give her a nice turn of speed. (Courtesy owner James Cleary)

Morgan 382/3/4

If there is one thing that can vouch for the Morgan 382 as an excellent and affordable cruiser, it is the fact that it is found in every book on the subject. In researching the literature to determine if another book on affordable sailboats had any merit, it was clear to me that recent downshifts in pricing had made heretofore inaccessible boats much easier to purchase. But I also found the Morgan consistently on all the lists, including from respected authors like John Kretschmer, Gregg Nestor, and virtually every writer who has ever submitted a "best cruisers" list.

So while this selection does not cover any new ground, with almost 500 out there it would be unfair to leave out this great design. We refer to it as the 382, which was the new designation in 1977 after the original Charley Morgan design was completely revised by Ted Brewer and Jack Corey. But we talk in general terms about all the incarnations, meaning the 383 (1980) and finally the 384 (1983).

I am based in California, and there are not as many Morgans out here as there are closer to the original factory location in Florida. However, since the boat did not have excessive draft or beam, they were easily trucked, and there were quite a few sold on the Left Coast. I have been aboard at least three that I can recall, and have seen various others in cruising anchorages. They have always struck me as everything a 38-foot cruising boat should look like.

But don't let the 5-inch bulwarks and boxy trunk cabin fool you. Ted Brewer knows how to draw a slippery underbody, and the Morgan I sailed on in San Francisco Bay had no trouble keeping up with any other 38 out there, at least on a beam reach. In fact the boat was originally marketed as a "two-fer" racer-cruiser. But with the very shippy deck layout, skeg rudder, and encapsulated ballast instead of a bolt-on keel, more cruisers than racers gravitated toward the design.

Although I have two boys and tend to favor at least 40 feet to cruise, I must admit that, if I was single- or doublehanding, the 382 would be a finalist for my Goldilocks cruising boat. Down below she is big

enough but not so wide that you cannot work your way from handhold to handhold while heeled. There is enough teak everywhere to feel yachty, but with a white overhead she is not overly dark. The quality of the woodwork is good for an American yard, and the earlier boats do not use just the thin veneers of some later designs.

At sea you are almost certainly going to use whatever settee is to leeward to sleep, or perhaps the quarter berth if it is not being used as a garage. The V-berth on some models was conventional; other models had the over-under diagonally opposed singles. Both types were well ventilated via a big hatch. Depending on the weather, V-berths typically can be a bit boisterous on passages. For those who have convinced themselves that they need a separate private aft cabin, you will have to look else-

Years Produced	1977–1985
Designer	Ted Brewer/Jack Corey
Estimated Hulls Produced	500
Length Overall	38 feet 3 inches
Length at Waterline	30 feet 6 inches
Draft (shoal/deep keel)	5 feet/6 feet
Beam	12 feet
Sail Area	667 square feet
Capsize Number	1.81
Sail Area/Displacement Ratio	16
Displacement/Length Ratio	283
Displacement	18,000 lbs.
Ballast	6,800 lbs.
Typical Engine	Yanmar 27 hp
Fuel Capacity	40 gallons
Water Capacity	55 gallons
Typical Price Range	$25,000–$40,000 USD
Owners Association(s)	www.morgan38.org

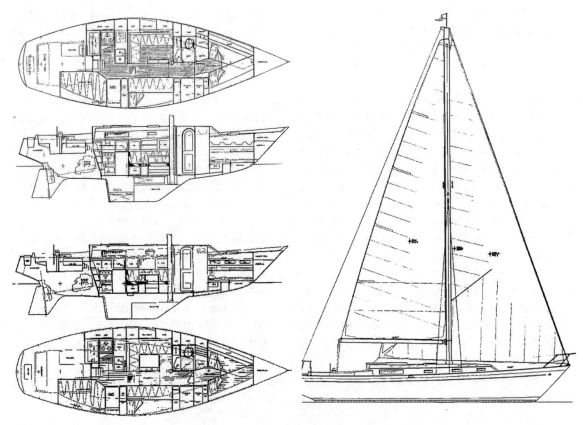

The simple elegance of the Morgan 382 sums up everything that cruising sailors are looking for in a couple's cruiser. The skeg rudder and 5-inch bulwarks for safe movement on deck are often cited as important factors in their popularity. (Courtesy Morgan/Catalina Yachts)

where. Ventilation was reported by some owners to be a problem on the stock 382 and improved on the last two versions. But I especially like the large head and shower stall, which was especially commodious in the earlier production years.

One of the things I have always liked about these Morgans is that they are not underpowered or underrigged. The majority of the boats came with the 50 horsepower Perkins 4-108, which is an engine I've seen on 45-footers. The deck cleats and chocks are oversized and well bedded. The mast was typically a Kenyon 6092 anodized spar, a cross section that is stan-

dard on the Hylas 44 and Celestial 48. In the earliest model years, writer John Kretschmer, in his *Used Boat Notebook*, points out some issues that were ultimately resolved.

"Early 382s did not have the aft head bulkhead glassed to the hull. This bulkhead helps support the mast partners and keeps the spar from working. In some of these boats, the keel was literally lowered by the compressive load of the pumping mast. To its credit, Morgan recalled those boats and resolved the problem by properly bonding the bulkheads to the hull.

Another early problem was the port forward lower chainplate, or lack thereof. Instead of a chainplate, the shroud was secured with a U-bolt, which tended to lift the deck and cause delamination. Many owners retrofitted chainplates and filled the delaminated deck area with epoxy."

Given that over thirty years have elapsed, these issues would almost certainly have been resolved on any boat you might be considering. These were single-spreader rigs, and the main shrouds have always been securely anchored into structural members down below and not on deck. As mentioned, the mast was anodized, which I personally prefer to reduce maintenance and constant linear polyurethane touchups. Painted masts will inevitably bubble up in some spots.

The boat has a small companionway, which is safer offshore than big loose hatchboards, and usually was accessed via some handy split doors. On the 382 and most 383s, the bridgedeck leading to the companionway also supported the mainsheet traveler, which makes for some limitations on a dodger installation. On the 384, the traveler was moved to the coachroof. Both the 383 and 384 sported a significantly higher-aspect rig than the 382, as well as a deeper rudder and the option of a 6-foot draft.

The cockpit is the typical T-layout, and the 382 had a very flat and boxlike helmsman's seat and a natural wood hatch that required maintenance. By the time the 384 came along, this was a nicely curved fiberglass surface that was comfortable on a heel.

But there is one thing that might lead a buyer to favor the earliest 382s over the models that followed: The hulls on some of the first 382s were made of solid fiberglass.

All the later hulls on the 383s and 384s are cored. Although all the Morgans across their entire production run had cored decks, it was only the first few years of the 382 that the boat had solid glass layups on the hull. For the solid glass purists out there, this can be a significant factor. As a surveyor, frankly I would not rule out a cored hull if I had checked it out carefully, but I understand the hesitation that some buyers may have, and it is a point worth considering.

There were some negative comments by owners I contacted regarding downwind tracking with the 382, which had a shorter rudder and keel than the later versions. She was a bit skittish, commented one owner, but he also said he had owned his 382 for over twenty years and overall was very happy with his choice. Close hauled, the boat sails beautifully. My several experiences on San Francisco Bay were always impressive and were usually sailed in a stiff chop.

The Good, the Bad, and the Ugly

I love the deck layout on this boat, especially the secure feeling when going forward along the wide side decks braced by a 5-inch gunwale. The caprail gives the boat a salty look but without the teak deck maintenance of the Tayana 37. The interior sports almost fifty lockers or bins for excellent cruising stowage. Unlike many other boats, she is not underpowered with the Perkins engine option. There is a strong owners association, with over 500 built. This boat definitely passes the test when you row away from her in an anchorage. Her lines will set your heart aflutter.

Many owners mentioned that the 383 and 384 were much better ventilated than the 382, something to consider unless your 382 has had some improvements.

In the Ugly department, some of the 382s used the same fire-retardant resin that caused the Valiant/Uniflite blister problems. Fortunately the recipe at the Florida factory must have been a little different, because although some Morgans have blisters, they did not suffer the same level of pox that the Valiants did. Lastly, the traveler arrangement on many versions makes a dodger installation difficult.

Owner Comments

"My boat, the Jenny Gordon, *carried a hull numbered 595195 and was a 1978 constructed vessel with a solid hull and an Airex cored deck. My hull drew 6 feet, and the rudder was a bit shorter in depth than the keel. The skeg-hung unit was hinged with a lower gudgeon about a foot above the bottom of the skeg with a built-in "give-away" or sacrificial skeg tip and rudder base apparently designed to give you something to get home with in the event of a rudder grounding and pounding. I thought it a clever means of constructing a pretty bulletproof rudder assembly and differed from the similarly underbodied Pacific Seacraft designed by Bill Crealock. Crealock hinged his rudder off a similarly sized skeg-hung rudder with a heavy bronze shoe serving as the lower gudgeon on the skeg tip of his design. I never had an incident that would have tested the giveaway portion of my boat, but I felt that the Brewer design afforded a great deal of security in that critical yet vulnerable area of the vessel.*

"I have heard the rumors that some other owners of the 382-4 thought the

Morgan 382 Dana *at anchor. Note the mast steps, dodger, bimini, radar, and davits. A boat being cruised locally but capable of going much farther if desired. (Courtesy James Cleary)*

rudders were undersized, but I put thousands and thousands of miles on my hull and never felt that the boat was in any way unbalanced or rudder-surface insufficient. My boat balanced effortlessly and did so in a wide variety of wind and sea conditions, and points of sail. My 382, with a 6-foot draft, sailed to weather like a high-performance racer, and the inboard shrouds allowed a good high point with closely hauled sails. Never did I feel she needed more rudder than she was designed with. What's more, when I was in the stink with many days of 45 to 65 knot winds sailing between the North Island of New Zealand and New Caledonia, I hove her to for three successive nights of extreme wind and sea conditions. With a triple-reefed main and a handkerchief-sized jib remaining on the Profurl roller furling, the boat handling went from surfing down waves to bobbing safely like a cork once the helm was thrown over, the jib back winded, and the helm locked down with the factory wheel lock. The rudder was completely adequate to keep the main driving up into the back-winded jib, and the vessel rode so comfortably in high seas that I went below, turned on the anchor light, made a call on the VHF to all vessels, and caught some safe and comfortable sleep."

—Christopher Cournoyer, owner
Jenny Gordon

The Cal 39 Dagmar at speed in the Marquesas Islands, French Polynesia. The only thing better than a day like this is having a buddy boat to take the shot. (Courtesy James Thomson)

Cal 39

It was halfway up the Baja peninsula, on a delivery, that I began to really appreciate the Cal 39. The infamous afternoon winds had just kicked in north of Cedros Island, and when it started to blow a consistent 28 knots I decided to tuck in behind tiny Isla San Jeronimo. As I sat at anchor watching the kelp leaves flap on the surface of the water (a sure indicator that we had 30 knot gusts in the anchorage), I spotted a lone sailboat about three miles offshore. It appeared to be under pure sail—a rarity for boats bucking north in those parts.

Hearing them on the VHF, I mentioned where I was and how impressive it was to see them out there charging into 6-foot, wind-frothed seas. They responded by saying they appreciated the compliment but were thinking about flopping over onto a port tack and heading for my spot, an anchorage few cruisers seemed willing to try due to Sacramento Reef.

"The reef is no problem," I told them. "Tack over and head straight for my boat. I can see you clearly and can guide you in."

As they approached I could see they were using a blade jib and a double-reefed main, perfectly trimmed. The boat was heeled over and charging hard. It was clear that this

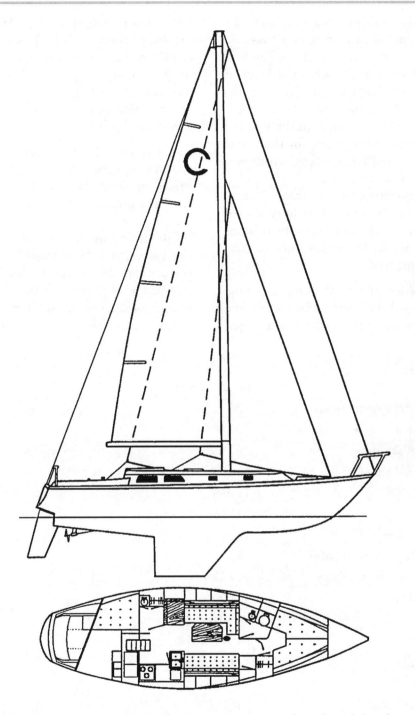

The Cal 39 with the Mark III interior, which offered a private quarter cabin. The sail plan shows an inner forestay, which was a rare factory option for those who wanted a cutter rig. (Courtesy Cal Owners Association)

cruising couple knew what they were doing. They anchored with nary a fuss or a cross word, and an hour later the crew of *Alaskan Spirit* was on board the Fleming 50 powerboat that I was skippering (my heart is in sail, but the money is in power). They were a retired couple in their sixties and had nothing but praise for their boat and where it had taken them, which was all over the Eastern Pacific.

In researching this chapter, I came across the original sales brochure for the Cal 39, and it made for interesting reading. Thirty years after the words were written, they still ring true.

"Some builders today think a plush interior is all it takes to make a boat a cruiser. Others seem to think a cruiser is an over-heavy boat designed before 1890. At Cal we don't believe in fads. To us a cruiser is a modern boat designed, from the bottom up, for cruising. A boat with a cabin built for onboard living, not just for dockside entertaining. And a hull designed to hold a course at sea for hours on end."

Sign me up! No wonder Bill Lapworth was held in such high regard. You can pick pretty much any boat he designed and find satisfied owners out there cruising with them.

Jack Jensen hired Bill Lapworth in the early 1960s, and their first boat was the popular Cal 24. Jensen Marine quickly grabbed a lot of market share as the reputation of their breakthrough Cal 40 grew as an ocean racer. Bangor Punta Marine

Years Produced	1978–1986
Designer	Bill Lapworth
Estimated Hulls Produced	200
Length Overall	39 feet
Length at Waterline	32 feet
Draft (shoal/deep keel)	5 feet 6 inches/6 feet 8 inches
Beam	12 feet
Sail Area	721 square feet
Capsize Number	1.8
Sail Area/Displacement Ratio	17.5
Displacement/Length Ratio	232
Displacement	17,000 lbs.
Ballast	7,000 lbs.
Typical Engine	Perkins 50 hp
Fuel Capacity	45 gallons
Water Capacity	130 gallons
Typical Price Range	$38,000–$55,000 USD
Owners Association(s)	www.cal39.info
Owner Blog	http://www.sailblogs.com/member/sailingthepacific/

The Cal 39 Dagmar *at anchor on remote Beveridge Reef in the South Pacific. The relatively high-aspect-ratio rig and large sail area make this boat a great performer. (Courtesy James Thomson)*

bought Jensen around 1965, though the factory stayed in Costa Mesa. But in 1980, production moved to Tampa, and more Cals were then sold on the East Coast than in the state they were named for.

It may well be that the Cal 34 ended up being their most popular cruiser since so many were made, but the 39 still looks good today, with some important differences over the 34, 36, and 40 that came earlier. The original Cal 39 came out in 1971 but was much more spartan than the Mark II, which began production in 1978. The Mark II came with standard diesel power and a much-updated interior, and later was even available with a quarter cabin. According to information found on the Cal 39 website put together by Wayne Gillikin, there were about 184 Mark IIs built without the quarter cabin, and at least 34 built with the aft cabin option. The Mark III was the last Cal 39 incarnation and was available only with the quarter cabin.

The interior is typical for American production boats of its day, with enough teak to give it warmth but not so much as to create a cave-like gloom. The shower was integrated into the head compartment in most layouts—not unusual but, for some buyers, not as desirable as a separate shower stall. Personally I prefer to give up the separate shower stall in order to get a real aft cabin into 39 feet.

Stowage options are excellent, with almost no interior space going to waste or being impossible to access. The mast is keel stepped but unobtrusive as it is placed next to a main bulkhead forward. The chart table on most models has the swing-out stool seen on the Newport 41 and other racer-cruisers popular at the time. In some interiors the end of a settee doubles as the seat for the navigation station.

Some might criticize the positioning of the shrouds, which are in the middle of the side decks and slightly difficult to get around when one is moving forward. But the reality is that placing the chainplates at the extreme beam of the boat limits the sheeting angles on many designs, and I personally did not find their placement problematic. The rigging load is transferred through the deck to structural members down below, and the installation is quite adequate.

This boat usually is available on the used market and sometimes at incredible prices. It has always been on my short list of boats to look for if I ever decide to take up the call once more and head out cruising again. Thanks to Hollywood, however, there are now two fewer available. A total of three were purchased for use in the Robert Redford film *All Is Lost*, and two of them were destroyed during the filming.

The Good, the Bad, and the Ugly

There is not much ugly about this design, but there is a consensus that the Perkins- or Yanmar-equipped boats are to be preferred over those that still have a Pathfinder diesel. Also, at almost 7 feet loaded for cruising, the deep-draft version may be problematic for East Coast owners. Some owners reported that they had replaced their hollow-shaft spade rudders after about twenty years, though it seemed it was more from rusting rather than a catastrophic failure.

The boat had a solid fiberglass hull, but the deck was balsa cored with some plywood inserted at high-load areas. As always, check for any wet core or delamination. If your surveyor brings a moisture meter to the survey, he or she should know how to establish a baseline reading

for the boat and can use that to see if some areas are showing high readings relative to the baseline.

Although Lapworth said that his favorite design was his 46, it is hard not to think that the 39 was his most refined design. You may also still see Cal 40s out there cruising, but the 39 has a much more efficient and modern interior. The size is perfect for a couple, the workmanship is good to excellent, and the sailing qualities are so good that the 39 is still sought out today by knowledgeable sailors who realize that Bill Lapworth was drawing fast but cruise-worthy boats long before anyone else.

Owner Profile, Dagmar

One such couple is James Thomson and Isabelle Chigros-Fraser, of Melbourne, Australia. They flew to the United States to buy their Cal 39 and then cruised it back to Australia, writing a great blog as well (http://www.sailblogs.com/member/sailingthepacific/).

"It was the adventure of a lifetime, and Dagmar was the perfect boat to make the crossing with," said James. "Not only does she sail well, but she is also a comfortable and trusty home."

Their blog is beautifully done, and James is quick to reply to e-mail inquiries about his Cal. It is worth noting that there are many Kiwis and Aussies flying to the U.S. West Coast because they are finding tremendous values in quality-built performance cruisers like the Cal 39. As this book went to press, there was a 1980 tall rig Cal 39 for sale in Honolulu with a Perkins diesel, Profurl, a new dodger, an Aries windvane, radar, an SSB, a life raft, and more—for $35,000.

Jeremy Alinson's O'Day 39 Forever Young, *en route to Madagascar from the Chagos Archipelago. The O'Day 39 and 40 were the largest boats built under that brand, and with proper planning can make impressive passages. (Courtesy Fatty Goodlander sailing on* Wild Card)

O'Day 39/40

For whatever reason, perhaps because the name O'Day was associated with smaller "day" sailors, the largest boat in their production history is almost never mentioned by the experts as being cruise-worthy. The accompanying photo, however, was taken after thousands of miles of bluewater cruising by Jeremy Alinson in his O'Day 39 *Forever Young*. He happened to be buddy boating with Fatty Goodlander on his well-traveled *Wild Card*, and Fatty snapped this great photo hundreds of miles off the coast of Madagascar. Not bad for a "day" sailing boat.

I have surveyed and sailed this boat. For budget cruisers I consider this a sleeper worth a look. They can be had for under $50,000 and will not seem out of place next to the newest designs being produced today, and they are more elegant than many. Like all the boats included in this book, however, the construction or design has some flaws, and each individual boat needs to be carefully examined by a surveyor prior to purchase.

This was first a Philippe Briand design marketed as the Jeanneau Sun Fizz. The French rarely allow right angles anywhere in their designs, and she exhibits gently eased lines throughout. The cockpit in particular is well executed with ergonomic curves molded into the seats.

Years Produced	1978–1990
Designer	Phillipe Briand/Raymond Hunt
Estimated Hulls Produced	290
Length Overall	39 feet 6 inches (40 model adds swim platform)
Length at Waterline	33 feet 5 inches
Draft (shallow/deep keel)	4 feet 11 inches/6 feet 4 inches
Beam	12 feet 6 inches
Sail Area	698 square feet
Capsize Number	1.92
Sail Area/Displacement Ratio	16
Displacement/Length Ratio	215
Displacement	18,000 lbs.
Ballast	6,600 lbs.
Typical Engine	Universal 40 hp
Fuel Capacity	42 gallons
Water Capacity	70 gallons
Typical Price Range	$40,000–$50,000 USD (40-ft. price slightly higher)
Most Active Owners Association	www.iheartodays.com
Owner Blog	http://www.sailblogs.com/member/sailingthepacific/

Probably no one knows the Jeanneau version of this boat better than Peter and Jeanne Pockel, who nearly circumnavigated in their boat *Watermelon*.

"The O'Day 39 is a Jeanneau Sun Fizz that was made under license. They are available in both a three-cabin, two-head version (39) and a two-cabin, one-head version (40). They are offshore proven. I know of two that are currently offshore and have been to the Caribbean and Mexico several times. We own a 1982 three-cabin version and find it quite comfortable with our family of four. She is a great handling boat and sails very well. The construction is very good and on par with the European boats. Pre-1986 boats have a solid-core hull; later ones have a cored hull. We primarily sail in the Pacific Northwest (with large tides and currents and big seas!). I would not hesitate to take the family offshore in this boat."

The O'Day 39, like the Beneteau 38, manages to fit two quarter cabins aft. There is even a tiny head tucked in to starboard. It could be argued that, as long as nobody is over six feet in height, this 39 gets more out of its interior than any other boat out there. Three private cabins, two heads, and still a decent stowage locker in the cockpit all the way aft. On the 40 you get a small swim step molded into the transom (one of the first U.S. boats to incorporate this) and just one aft cabin, but the athwartships berth is queen sized, albeit a bit claustrophobic under the cockpit.

In my day sail on this design, it was clear that this boat could turn and burn with pretty much any design included in this book. But like the Newport 41 and the Islander 36, the original nonskid design molded into the deck is subject to wear, and if you buy a well-used model it is quite a project to try to duplicate the original nonskid pattern. Amateur efforts to match or renew the original nonskid will usually fall short, and therefore it is helpful to have an idea how much it might cost to have a pro renew the nonskid if the deck on yours is too slick for safe offshore work.

The boat has enough teak down below to give it a warm feel but not so much that things get dark or overly hard to maintain. These boats used the ubiquitous teak and holly veneer soles, but the veneer is subject to wear and you will want to see how the sole is holding up. Replacing these areas is not cheap, so my boys and I have learned long ago on our own boats that the shoes come off prior to going below.

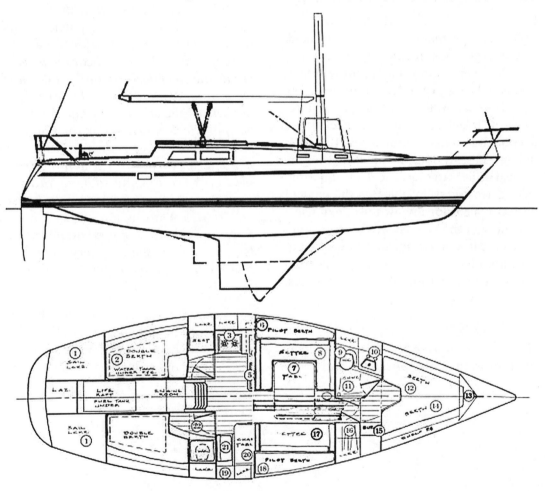

The O'Day 39 stuffed in three berth areas and two heads, while the 40 had two cabins and one head—more logical for a cruising couple. The primary thing to watch for on these boats is gelcoat cracking.

It takes only one pebble stuck in a shoe to scratch the devil out of a wood sole.

On both the 39 and the 40, the aft berths require a big sacrifice in terms of cockpit locker storage, so this design makes sense only if you are going to make good use of these berths. If you are a singlehander, or one of you feels a little claustrophobic tucked back under the cockpit, then this design may not be for you.

The Good, the Bad, and the Ugly

One thing to like about these boats, especially the 40, is that they do not look dated. The curved cockpit seating, sleek lines, and the swim platform all point to a boat that could have just rolled off the assembly line. They sail well and, although the interior is a bit lacking in stowage space, there is enough to make it cruiseable. Based on my own observations, I would say that the critical thing is to see if the deck and cabin sides gelcoat is still viable. On the model I almost bought for my own use, extensive checking in the gelcoat was starting, and replacing it was not a project I wanted to get into. I have seen other examples from the same year without the gelcoat issues, so don't give up.

Owner Comments

"I loved our quarter berths, and on overnight crossings and passages they were the best place to be. They were exceptionally comfortable no matter how bad the seas and weather are, and the porthole into the cockpit meant that the person on watch didn't have to leave the cockpit to call for help if necessary. I spoke with one couple with two young sons who bought the O'Day 39 with that layout, and they too loved it for those quarter berths, where each of their sons could have his own cabin.

"We once were beating our brains out in 50-knot winds, hove-to with the mainsail reefed all the way down, when a nastier gust blew out the mainsail. I was on watch; Peter didn't even hear the noise or feel the lurch of the boat until I called him. Of course, we had made the mistake of not setting the stormsail rather than just keeping the deeply reefed main. But in defense of our mistake, the conditions did not deteriorate until near midnight, and we didn't really want to be working on deck in such dark and nasty conditions.

"I miss Watermelon. We sold her in Singapore, and her new owners have kept her name. She was very good to us, and we have so many fond memories of our passages in her."

—Jeanne Pockel, Jeanneau Sun Fizz (precursor to the O'Day 39) *Watermelon:* http://www.cruiser. co.za/hostmelon.asp

David Risch's C & C 40 Corsair *at the start of the Marion-Bermuda race in 2009. Although some pundits avoid fully cored boats like these for cruising, a careful survey should reveal if there are any serious issues, and if the verdict is good you may find yourself with an able cruiser that will leave the crab crushers well behind. (Courtesy David Risch)*

C & C 40

There are plenty of "industry experts" or forum rats who are dismissive of any former IOR racer-cruiser as a serious bluewater boat, especially if it had all balsa core construction. I'll admit I have seen some saturated cored decks that resembled trampolines and others with winches that, under sail, started to heel as the load deflected the fiberglass beneath it. Those nightmares are out there, but a good surveyor will find core issues at survey, and aspiring cruisers on a budget would do well to consider the C & C 40. It is potentially much more than an obsolete 1980s racer-cruiser.

I suppose before continuing, some justification needs to be made as to why this chapter is on the C & C 40 and not the C & C Landfall 38—a boat that in theory was more intended for cruising. One reason is that the Landfall 38—a perfectly good boat—has been well covered in other publications. The other reason is that since both boats are balsa cored on the hull and deck, and sport fin keels and spade rudders, you might as well get the extra interior space on the less-sought-after 40. They are priced about the same, and the capsize screening factor is actually about the same—1.8 for the Landfall and 1.9 for the 40. In fact there is some evidence that the windows and

This is the hard-to-find aft-cabin version of the C & C 40. These are well-built boats and probably the best all-around sailer on The List. (Courtesy designer Rob Ball)

sight into the boat and its construction. I was able to reach lead designer Ball at his office with Edson Industries, and he had these comments:

"The 40 was one of my favorites because at the time it came out, it looked like it was marketing suicide. The New York Yacht Club was coming out with the New York 40, which they were pushing hard with lots of money, and on the Great Lakes they had the North American 40. But we went ahead anyway, and then on the race circuit we cleaned up against them."

Ball attributes a lot of this success to making sure the boat could be built to the designed weight—in other words that she would float on her lines once she came off the assembly line. "It doesn't do any good to design a superlight boat if the factory is not going to end up building it to that specification," he told me. "I spent a lot of time figuring what weight the 40 could be built to, and she came out exactly as planned." Technically Ball was also trying to draw a boat for the IOR rule, but he did not go to the extremes that some designers did. The boat was reasonably competitive under IOR, but it did better when the later IMS (International Measurement System) handicap system became popular in the mid-1980s.

But of course speed is relatively low on the priority list of many cruisers, and the reason I think this boat deserves a look goes well beyond her ability to beat your buddy boat to the next anchorage.

Maybe a quick list of attributes would help. The boat has a true bridgedeck and a bluewater-appropriate small companionway entry (the earlier models were more dodger-friendly). She came standard with

deck fittings were less prone to leaks on the 40 than the 38.

By the time Rob Ball penned the 40, he was well established as a designer who knew how to draw for speed. The lines of the 40 reflect the wide, relatively flat bottom that made this boat really scoot and collect a ton of trophies, and she is competitive even today. I had the pleasure of interviewing both Rob Mazza and Rob Ball for this chapter, and they gave a lot of in-plenty of self-tailing winches, usually a Yanmar diesel, a full-beam settee, and an efficient galley. The steering and running gear were first quality, and these boats typically have an excellent sail inventory and electronics package. Earlier models had a spacious aft bunk, and then a separate aft cabin in the final production run.

"The last twelve built had a private aft cabin to compete with the French boats that were coming out," explains designer Ball. *"There were also ten or eleven built with a centerboard for the Marblehead fleet. All told, 126 hulls were made."*

The centerline full-beam saloon table means you can have six people seated comfortably at once. That capacity will not be needed under way, but most cruisers get pretty social, and if you have invited over two other couples, it is nice to have the same seating capacity as a 45-footer. You may also find that only half the table is "deployed" and useable at sea on a given tack, usually the downhill or leeward side. Experienced cruisers who remember working on their laptops on passages know all about "tacking" the saloon table on this sort of centerline design.

The finish quality is good to excellent. I personally don't like an all-teak cave inside, and prefer the lighter and more open feel of wood accents over primarily fiberglass surfaces. Most of these boats had four hanging lockers and plenty of stowage, so this was not a minimalist racing interior. The 40 had a huge foredeck hatch installed as standard. When the boat is anchored, this really helps to get airflow started aft and out the companionway.

Years Produced	1977–1989
Designer	Rob Ball/C & C Design Group
Estimated Hulls Produced	126
Length Overall	39 feet 7 inches
Length at Waterline	31 feet 6 inches
Draft (centerboard/deep keel)	4 feet 11 inches/7 feet
Beam	12 feet 7 inches
Sail Area	743 square feet
Capsize Number	1.9
Sail Area/Displacement Ratio	17.9
Displacement/Length Ratio	244
Displacement	17,100 lbs.
Ballast	7,910 lbs.
Typical Engine	Yanmar 34 hp
Fuel Capacity	20 gallons
Water Capacity	70 gallons
Typical Price Range	$40,000–$57,000 USD
Most Active Owners Association	www.cncphotoalbum.com

In reviewing all the caveats included here about a cored boat, you may, gentle reader, be sufficiently terrified that you simply stay away from the cored boats on The List. That would be a mistake, especially if you really like to sail. For one thing, a lot of cruising is done in light winds, and the C & C can keep moving in light airs when a Taiwan Teakie is rolling gunwale to gunwale or motoring in a cloud of its own diesel exhaust. The 40 has the shrouds well inboard for excellent sheeting angles, and there is a lot to be said for a boat that can manage 4 knots when the wind is barely rippling the water. It helps morale and also means much less schlepping of jerry jugs upon landfall.

But you should certainly go into a potential purchase with your eyes wide open and a knowledgeable surveyor working for you. Rob Mazza was the senior designer at C & C who specialized in spars, rigs, structures, and deck layouts. He also spent a lot of time sailing C & C custom and production boats at the SORC, the Bermuda Races, Admirals Cup, Canada's Cup, and more. He comments, "The genoa tracks are an area to check carefully since they can see significant loading that may shift fasteners and affect watertightness. And if the boat had ever grounded hard, you need to see if there is any sign of stress cracks in the bilges around the keel attachment."

The Good, the Bad, and the Ugly

This is a sweet-sailing boat that will probably go by any other cruiser on The List. Its PHRF (Performance Handicap Racing Fleet) rating is 108, and it has a nicely done interior. They are out there at some excellent prices because of the online gossip saying that you should never consider a cored boat for cruising. But if you find one that has been cared for, and you continue to do the same, this can be a fantastic opportunity. If nothing else, the sail inventory and electronics package will usually be excellent. The engine access is good, and it is also possible to find a boat that has seen only freshwater. Trucking costs would apply.

As Corsair *charges along on a starboard tack, note the clean wake and sweet lines. Designer Rob Ball felt that this was the best boat he ever created, and most would have to agree. (Courtesy David Risch)*

One unfortunate reality is that the resale value for these boats may always be lower than that of other "traditional" cruisers since, whether fair or not, these boats are pigeonholed as outdated IOR racers with potential core issues. But that also has its advantages for savvy buyers like you!

The ugly would be that, as far as I can see, in some model years (especially 1982 and 1983) this is a difficult boat on which to mount a dodger, and I personally would never cruise without a dodger and bimini. Also, due to the babystay, it may be difficult to carry an inverted dinghy on the foredeck, and I don't recommend davits. Fuel tankage was only 20 gallons and would probably need to be doubled for serious cruising, or at least you should be prepared to festoon the decks with yellow jerry jugs.

Comments from Designer Rob Ball and Owner David Risch

"There are people obsessed with the whole core issue, including a lot of panic when it first was becoming apparent. There is a big difference between some moisture in the core and a true structural problem from saturation. In many ways this core was overbuilt, and you can safely sail anywhere with some moisture in it, but it is also possible to find 40s that have no issues at all. Check especially if a speedometer was installed forward because these were not done at the factory, and I have seen some causing a saturated core.

The bottom line is that these boats are a tremendous value. They cost less than a third of, say, a Sabre 36 but offer a bigger cruising interior and usually a great equipment list."

—Rob Ball, chief designer of the C & C 40

From veteran owner and racer David Risch, here are the boat's best attributes.

- *Sweetest sailing boat on all points of sail except when pressed hard under a chute*
- *Great cockpit design, especially for the helmsman*
- *With the flag blue/white color combo, she turns heads everywhere she goes*
- *Easily balanced and easily driven*
- *A real offshore interior (pilot berths/handholds, etc.) with a properly sized galley and nav station*
- *Fast in light air*
- *Handles well offshore in storm conditions*
- *Quality build throughout*
- *All-wood handcrafted interior*

And the worst . . .

- *Small tankage (60 gallons of water and 20 gallons of diesel)*
- *Interior is not as friendly as modern interiors*
- *7 foot 6 inch draft occasionally limits cruising ground*
- *All-wood interior is beautifully finished but a bit dark*

The Mark II version of the Newport 41 had larger windows and a higher profile on the trunk cabin, and she sported a longer waterline. (Courtesy www.capitalyachts.info)

Newport 41

Back in the mid-1980s, I was living in Monterey, California, when a local dentist put out the word that he needed rail meat for a Wet Wednesday race. Eager to get into racing, and because I had the entry level skill required to be able to move on command from one side of the boat to the other, I was glad when told that my rail meat offer had been accepted. After battling our way through the sea lions that crawl all over the marina docks there, I spotted the gleaming blue hull of a Newport 41, the first one I had ever seen.

This, I thought to myself, is what a sailboat is supposed to look like.

She appeared to be moving at 7 knots just sitting at her slip. The new self-tailing winches gleamed, and at the helm was the biggest wheel I had ever seen on a production boat that size. As we left the harbor and I stowed my things down below, I took a quick glance around a very appealing interior. I saw a nice nav station to starboard as I came down the companionway ladder. Just enough wood was used to give the interior some character but not make it too dark. The galley was easily managed in a seaway. Although we were racing that day, I could easily see myself on board that boat about halfway to Puerta Vallarta in cruising mode.

As usual out on Monterey Bay, a big swell was running as the storm seas off Alaska pushed their energy southward. At the top of the swell we would get about 20 knots of wind, and in the trough 5 knots less. The Newport loped along easily, with the helmsman rarely needing more than two fingers on the wheel.

Later on the downwind leg, we managed to set the chute . . . sideways. This was something I did not even know was possible until that afternoon. At least the owner's son was at fault and the rail meat was not blamed, but the amazing thing was that the spinnaker actually flew at all. The cockpit team decided to leave it up for an embarrassing twenty minutes.

Given the long production run of this boat, I was certainly not the only one impressed with its design. It was first produced by C & C Yachts of Canada, and optimized to the old CCA Rule. The Cruising Club of America design parameters tended to avoid some of the extremes that sometimes afflicted the later racing conventions such as the IOR. The direct precursor to the Newport 41 was the Redline 41 *Condor*, winner of the prestigious SORC regatta in 1972. In fact C & C (named for the original partners George Cuthbertson and George Cassian) was a remarkable success story for a Canadian company that took on the big U.S. companies and outlasted most of them. The racer-cruiser was their hallmark, and it is hard to find a model in the dozens they produced that could be termed ugly, or slow.

But despite the C & C 41 being a commercial success, the company sold the molds to California boatbuilders, and they

Years Produced	1978–1990 (includes Mark II)
Designer	C & C Yachts/Capital Yachts
Estimated Hulls Produced	190
Length Overall	41 feet
Length at Waterline	30 feet/32 feet (Mark II)
Draft	6 feet
Beam	11 feet 3 inches
Sail Area	750 square feet
Capsize Number	1.71
Sail Area/Displacement Ratio	17
Displacement/Length Ratio	245
Displacement	18,000 lbs.
Ballast	8,215 lbs.
Typical Engine	Universal 35–44 hp diesel
Fuel Capacity	40 gallons
Water Capacity	80 gallons
Typical Price Range	$30,000–$58,000 USD
Most Active Owners Association	www.capitalyachts.info

eventually landed in the hands of Capital Yachts, near Los Angeles, around 1972. Only subtle improvements were made until the early 1980s, when the Mark II came out with an extended rudder and bustle that added 2 feet to the waterline. The cabin trunk was slightly higher, and some deck modifications were made, but the overall performance was almost unchanged. Some owners who had sailed both models reported that the Mark II tracked better with the new rudder configuration.

There were two interior options available on the later boats, shown here. To my mind, if only a couple were crewing, either version would be fine, but if crewed by a family or more than one couple, the tri cabin is probably more desirable. I like the bigger dinette table on the traditional interior, but I also think the privacy of the tri-cabin design is a plus.

The designers specified a rare offset engine installation, which is to port under the aft part of the settee. Access is fairly good once the furniture is removed. By using this location, the usual engine compartment under the companionway is completely open, and cruisers like those on *One Flew Blue*—a Newport 41 that sailed to New Zealand—practically gush about how much stowage they have underneath the cockpit.

The engine itself varied over the long production run, but generally Yanmars were on the earlier boats and Universal Diesels (a Kubota block) were typical on later boats. The 35 horsepower version was just enough to push the boat since the long prop shaft robbed some juice before it made it to the prop. The boats that came with more horsepower are preferable, but it is an easily driven hull design in any event.

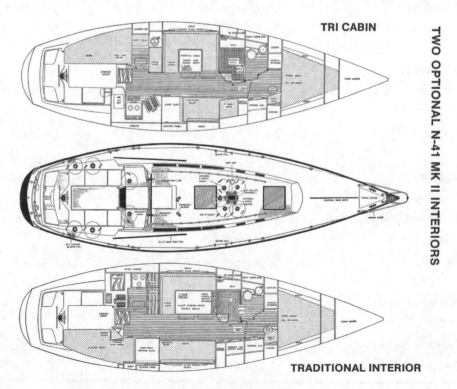

TRI CABIN

TWO OPTIONAL N-41 MK II INTERIORS

TRADITIONAL INTERIOR

The quality of the finish is more than adequate. The bulkhead tabbing needs to be checked if the boat has been sailed hard, but there have never been any wholesale blister issues as on some other makes and models. Certainly the most critical area for inspection is the balsa-cored deck. The hull itself is overbuilt solid glass, but the deck on these boats will be over 30 years old and should be surveyed at the time of purchase by someone experienced. The hull-deck joint seems to have avoided problems, but some owners had to replace or rebed chainplates and occasionally repair a compromised core in the deck.

The overall strength of these boats is impressive, and many owners say that the best thing about the boat is the "Cadillac ride." Several of these boats have cruised from the West Coast to New Zealand or Australia, and I would venture to guess that some folks went all the way around, although I was unable to find out who they are. There are actually quite a few people out there who circumnavigate and choose not to write a book about it!

Given that virtually any Newport 41 will be at least 30 years old, it is worth saying that the wiring should have been replaced or you will have to budget a pretty big number to do so yourself. If the plumbing is still 1970s original, you will want to factor that in as well.

The Good, the Bad, and the Ugly

The 41 offers great sailing performance despite the long overhangs that shorten the waterline length. Owners comment on the stiffness and solid feel even if the boat is working hard to weather. In light air the boat, at 18,000 pounds displacement, will take a while to get in gear. It has a spacious feel below. It is not overly dark like some

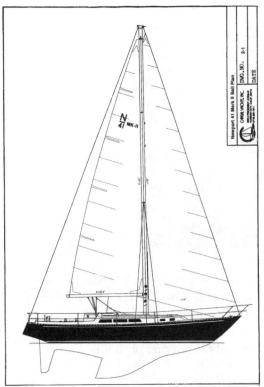

Sail plan (above) and interior options (opposite page) for the Newport 41. If you value privacy or will have more than a couple aboard, the tri cabin is nice, but it does not offer the cook as much safety while under way as the traditional layout. (Courtesy www.capitalyachts.info)

Taiwanese boats but still offers nice teak accents and veneers.

If the boat has been heavily used, the nonskid pattern on the deck, which was not very aggressive to begin with, may be worn away. This would mean either painting the decks and applying a new nonskid pattern (expensive) or being very careful at sea.

Some owners commented that due to the offset prop shaft, the boat had a mind of its own in reverse. If you intend to spend a lot of time in marinas, this may be a minor issue since one can usually plan a

The Newport 41 Mark II Summerwind *slips along off Newport Beach, California, in typically light conditions. The mainsheet tackle in the cockpit is far enough aft for a dodger but makes a bimini problematic. Other versions used a traveler on the coachroof. (Courtesy owner Brian Smith and www.capitalyachts.info)*

marina departure fairly easily for reversing issues and plan accordingly with a human bow thruster or two.

Ugly? The Newport 41 is many things, but ugly is not one of them.

Owner Comments

"We bought our N41 after a number of years chartering many different boats. Took input from each member of the family to work up a list of desired features. A large cockpit that is still workable offshore was a key need. While we often sail with six or seven, we shorthand with two. It's divided at the steering pedestal in a way that works well for both cruising and racing with a crowd.

"A view out the cabin was valuable to avoid a 'down in the pit' feeling. The N41 lower freeboard with a slightly taller trunk cabin works well. Interior is just three steps down from the cockpit. The interior doesn't have the 'wide open ballroom' issues of some volumized boats, however the boat still feels spacious because nothing was miniaturized during the design.

"Separate shower next to the head, big galley, and engine access under the settee L are great. In addition to the cockpit lazarette, there is a huge open storage area under the entire cockpit.

"We wanted a smooth and easy motion because one of the family has some susceptibility to motion sickness. Found a spreadsheet that compared 1,100 boats using Marchaj's research on crew effectiveness, g-forces, and motion that helped our search be successful. The boat has a more easily driven hull than some of the wide boats out now. The stern is fuller aft than the pinched IOR style, yet the rudder stays in the water when heeled. Moderate overhangs. Deck generally dry in seas over three feet (drier than other boats we tried). Good coamings on cockpit keep deck water out even at high angles of heel."

—Paul McQuillan, owner 1983
Newport 41 Mark II

The Golden Wave 42
Born Free *anchored at Mayaguana in the Bahamas. At 42 feet, this is the biggest boat on our list. (Courtesy John Trayfors)*

Golden Wave 42

The Golden Wave 42 is a remarkable boat designed by the person responsible for more refined performance cruisers than any other yacht designer in history—Robert Perry. Sadly only about a hundred of this incredible boat were built, so it barely made The List. I had the opportunity to sail one out of Santa Barbara several times, and like all Perry designs she was a sweetly balanced performer with the best interior, in my opinion, a cruising couple could ever ask for.

It is almost stunning to consider that these boats can be had for around $50,000, but they can. I found three between $49,000 and $59,000 in a YachtWorld search. More than anything else, the price is probably because of the teak decks, done "old style" with hundreds of screws and plugs, which can indeed be a pain but also the salvation for anyone willing to look past any deck issues to the bones beneath. A little sweat equity and you can have an incredible cruiser that can keep up with almost anything else in its size range.

It was around 1980 that Cheoy Lee yachts of Hong Kong put the word out that they were seeking design submittals for the ultimate 42-footer, an ideal size for a couple to handle with comfort and safety. At the time, Bob Perry

Years Produced	1981–1988
Designer	Robert Perry
Estimated Hulls Produced	100
Length Overall	42 feet
Length at Waterline	34 feet 4 inches
Draft	6 feet 2 inches
Beam	12 feet 8 inches
Sail Area	885 square feet (genoa)
Capsize Number	1.71
Sail Area/Displacement Ratio	16.6
Displacement/Length Ratio	277
Displacement	25,000 lbs.
Ballast	9,484 lbs.
Typical Engine	Yanmar 3GM
Fuel Capacity	55 gallons
Water Capacity	120 gallons
Typical Price Range	$48,000–$65,000 USD
Owners Association(s)	www.cheoyleeassociation.com

was making his mark with breakthroughs like the Valiant 40, which he drew about six years earlier.

"The feel of the helm of the Golden Wave 42 must be experienced. She has a light definite touch that responds immediately. She moves smartly in the lightest of breezes and is strong enough to handle the roughest conditions. Close-hauled she is swift and keen and quick to come about, and before the wind in all her glory there are none that can compare."

Wow!

In all her glory there are none that can compare?

Perhaps a bit of over-the-top marketing hyperbole from a writer more familiar with Mandarin than English, but, hey, sign me up. The first time I took the helm of

a Golden Wave—on a sea trial that I was running on behalf of a yacht broker—I was certainly impressed. The deeper I dug into the details of the design, the more I liked it.

Subtle things like an off-center companionway can make for increased options in the accommodations below. By shifting the companionway to starboard just a foot, Perry allowed for a dedicated and capacious owner's cabin to port, complete with a separate shower stall instead of the usual "sit and soak" configuration when the showering occurs in the same compartment as the head. The bed is a true double. It's probably the best master stateroom you can get in this size of boat that can still sail.

Rather than cramming in more bunks or head compartments than necessary, it is clear that Perry was designing primarily for one couple aboard the Golden Wave. He specified just one head on the boat, but he makes it big, and does the same for the only real sea berth aft. In my opinion it makes for the best interior for a cruising couple I have seen in 42 feet.

At the bottom of the companionway to starboard, there is a nice nav station, and then going forward is the galley in an almost fore-and-aft layout along the starboard side. With the stateroom bulkhead just behind you, one has a convenient way to brace while cooking—or at the very least to minimize the distance that you might find yourself tossed around during rough seas.

The mast is keel stepped for strength but unobtrusive since the dinette table

The interior of the GW 42 was virtually unchanged during its production run. Note how the slightly off-center companionway allows for a nice aft cabin. (Courtesy Golden Wave Owners Association)

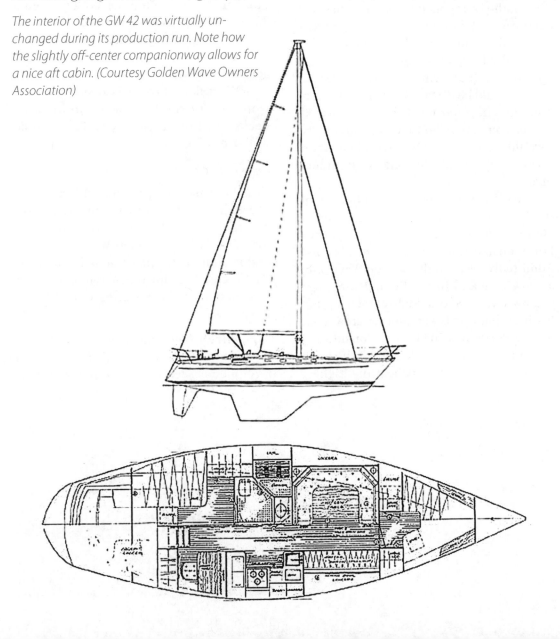

is beautifully wrapped around it, with the woodwork that Hong Kong yards are known for. Across from the dinette is a settee that is low enough to be a great sea berth. Forward on both sides of the boat is closet or drawer stowage before the ubiquitous V-berth (rarely used on passages).

The build quality on the boat is good, especially the woodwork. But in most cases if the boat you are looking at has not been rewired, you may see some voltage drop and conductivity issues. Most of the Taiwan-built boats represented here used non-marine grade wire, which, if never replaced, could be 30 years old. Try to determine just how hard it will be to rewire if in fact you may need to do so. Personally I would rather have to re-rig a boat than rewire it, due to all the joinery and liners involved.

Under sail this boat reminded me of the Passport 40 that I once singlehanded about a thousand miles. It was another Perry design that behaved impeccably. Admittedly I was on the Golden Wave only a few times and in mild conditions, but the owners I have talked to back up my instinct that this is yet another great boat off the Perry drawing board. Considering that it is usually available for half the price of a Passport, I give this boat my highest

ranking for a bargain cruiser that can be purchased—if you are a bit lucky and patient—for $50,000.

The Good, the Bad, and the Ugly

This is a 42-foot fiberglass diesel-powered Bob Perry designed performance cruiser with a gorgeous interior optimized for one couple. It is often priced less than a Tayana 37 (another Perry design) and has a much larger interior than that model.

The only bad is that this boat is no longer being made!

OK, it does have teak decks, but if it were not for the boats with failing teak decks, the price to get a GW 42 would be well over $50,000.

Owner Comments

This boat is often purchased by knowledgeable surveyors or captains who know a bargain when they see one. Bill Trayfors owns a 1981 Golden Wave, hull #17, and is an industry professional who owns YachtSense in Arlington, Virginia. He is an original owner and has cruised his GW extensively.

"I positively LOVE the boat. After 22 years of ownership, I can truthfully say that I have never seen a boat in her size that

Born Free anchored near the schooner Heritage in Maine. Designer Robert Perry gave the boat ample freeboard, which increased the space below. (Courtesy Bill Trayfors)

I'd rather have. She's a dream to sail. Handles beautifully in any weather. With the furling headsail and the boom-furling full-batten main, she's easy to sail from the cockpit, with no need to go forward for reefing.

"I have sailed her many thousands of miles from Maine to Grenada and most places in between. Eleven years in the Eastern Caribbean. Two summers in Maine. Several trips down the ICW to the Keys. Lots of sailing on home waters (Chesapeake Bay) and environs. I have not found the 6.5-foot draft to be a problem. There are just too many wonderful places to go that can easily accommodate that draft.

"Re construction, she was designed by Bob Perry and built by Cheoy Lee's Golden Wave Shipyards in Hong Kong (which I've visited several times). She was built to a high standard as an attempt to regain a bit of Cheoy Lee's reputation, employing U.S. and British hard-ware to a high degree. She had Navtec rod rigging originally, and a keel-stepped mast. I had her re-rigged in Tortola about ten years ago, using British steel 10 mm 1 × 19 s/s cable. Changed out all the chainplates and rigging screws, the bow pulpit and fittings, etc., etc.

"Originally had teak decks but these were thin and screwed down. Very hard to maintain after a few years in the Caribbean, so I had them removed and put eight coats of Awlgrip, including one coat of nonskid, over the fiberglass decks."

—Bill Trayfors, owner

"In a nutshell, I loved our Golden Wave 42 and would trade the Malo 38 we now have in a heartbeat! Everything about it was perfect in my eyes. Brad would disagree, but only on the issue of engine access."

—Linda Attaway and Brad Nelson, who lost a GW 42 in the South Pacific on a reef

Once she is eased into a reach and the centerboard is cranked about halfway up, there is little to slow down a P40. The owners association has developed a second-generation rudder that improves downwind handling. Note the expansive flush deck for dinghies or kayaks.

Pearson 40 (Honorable Mention)

One of my unwritten rules in putting together The List was to avoid having more than one model from a given manufacturer. However, if you really are looking for value in cruising boats under $50,000, it is hard to overlook either the Pearson 36-2 or the older Pearson 40. However, since the P40 ended production in 1981 with only 71 hulls made, the design must accept Honorable Mention status as outside the minimum number of hulls required to make The List.

There will be resistance from some who would not put a Pearson on any list, thinking that they, like the Hunter 37, just are "not strong enough for offshore work." The keels will fall off! The layup needs to be three layers stronger! The Pacific Seacraft 40 is a much bettter boat!

Yes, I agree, the Pacific Seacraft is a better 40-footer. If you have a quarter million dollars to buy one, plus enough left over to go cruising, then have at it. If your budget is more like $35,000 and you want a boat that will allow you to go before your joints take half an hour to get lubricated in the morning, then this boat is worth a look.

This design certainly got my attention the first time I saw one in Channel Islands Harbor, California. She had, to my eye, a very sexy look with a flush deck and burgundy stripes to help visually alleviate the high freeboard. The owner was on board, and I immediately went over to ask about it, and he confirmed that he loved the sailing performance and that she had a very cruisable interior. I ended up surveying one a few years later, and on the sea trial in moderate winds the boat performed just fine despite my omnipresent doubts about centerboards.

But to those who doubt the Pearson line in general, I can only remind them that they were pioneers in the industry with incredible early boats like the Pearson Triton, a 28-footer with several circumnavigations to its credit. To be sure, not all the boats they put out were consistent in build quality, but the P40 seemed to get special attention from Bill Shaw and the Pearson team.

They decided to try building their first boat ever with a cored hull, and in some ways she is overbuilt. There have been virtually no core issues, according to the strong owners association, and with a nicely cambered flush deck the overall structural strength is impressive. I am, unfortunately, north of 200 pounds, but the Pearson 40 that I walked on and surveyed had no flexing at all underfoot. The deck and hull are bonded together in seamless fashion to provide what is essentially a single massively strong shell that is further reinforced by interior bulkheads and joinery.

Years Produced	1977–1981
Designer	Bill Shaw/Pearson Yachts
Estimated Hulls Produced	71
Length Overall	40 feet
Length at Waterline	31 feet 4 inches
Draft (board up/board down)	4 feet 4 inches/9 feet 5 inches
Beam	12 feet 2 inches
Sail Area	750 square feet
Capsize Number	1.71
Sail Area/Displacement Ratio	16
Displacement/Length Ratio	327
Displacement	22,500 lbs.
Ballast	8,215 lbs.
Typical Engine	Westerbeke 37 hp diesel
Fuel Capacity	46 gallons
Water Capacity	90 gallons
Typical Price Range	$30,000–$50,000 USD
Most Active Owners Association	www.pearson40.net

And this boat can haul the mail. I did a few beer can races on the first one I ever saw, and even with a centerboard she pointed with every racer-cruiser out there. Once we rounded the windward buoy, we could raise the board halfway and crack off on a reach, passing almost everyone. With over half her displacement of 22,500 pounds in ballast, this is not an ultralight, but there is some initial tenderness as described by one owner below.

Some downwind squirreliness is not surprising on a boat with only a narrow centerboard for tracking ability. This is, of course, a significant negative about this design. She looks like she is a roller downwind, but I have not sailed it enough to say

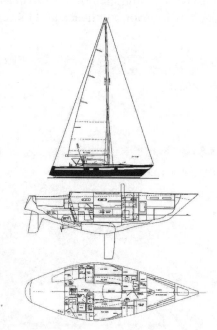

The distinctive underbody of the Pearson 40 was described as "whaleback"—not very different in profile than a humpback whale with the pectoral fin extended downward. Note the elegant dinghy stowage shown under the boom, safe in a seaway. (Courtesy Pearson 40 association www.Pearson40.net)

with certainty. I do know that the boat has been taken on some very significant passages. *Dreamcatcher* finished second in her class in the Victoria to Maui race. The owners website at www.pearson40.net has a complete owners roster and impressive info on the boat, with many upgrade and repair notes. Some owners actually got together and developed a Mark II rudder that helped with downwind control, which is described on the website.

Much is made of the "whale"-shaped hull, but for what I have seen, it can be described as a way to hydrodynamically fair in the centerboard slot, and it probably reduces turbulence. Whatever the case, the boat needs only a bit more than 4 feet of water to float. It does not appear that Pearson made, or even considered, a fixed-keel version of the boat. At the time, the Hood and Tartan centerboarders were popular, and this was in part a Pearson response to that success.

But Bill Shaw also wanted to ensure that the P40 interior was second to none, and although not quite living in the neighborhood of Hinckleys and Masons, it is indeed very nicely executed. Designer Bill Shaw wrote this in the original promotional literature.

"Below decks was fun to do. I sat down with my entire development team and challenged them to produce the kind of joinerwork, finish, and laminated woods that seem to have disappeared from the yachting scene, the kind that we tend to associate with custom yachts from some of the finest European yards. To say they met the challenge is an understatement. The interior of the new 40 is my and their proudest achievement in yacht finishing. Now that the 40 is a reality, in retrospect I have to say she's the complete yacht."

The Pearson 40 Passion *hauled out gives a good view of the unusual underbody bump at the centerboard trunk on this design. With the centerboard completely up, it is a good bet that tracking would decrease and rolling would increase. (Courtesy owner Chip Lawson)*

The main-strength bulkheads are beautifully curved and varnished. There is ash used as well as mahogany, and with the flush overhead the look and feel are completely different from those on any other 40-footer I have seen. At six feet two inches, I had just enough clearance throughout the cabin.

Ventilation in the tropics is critical, and the P40 takes advantage of its flush deck to provide hatches in places that normally have to be reserved for side decks or other footing. Of course these penetrations have been made into a balsa core, but the boat I saw had all balsa edges properly sealed and absolutely no delamination.

Owner Comments

"The Pearson 40 is definitely a nominally tender boat. Even though the P40 has better than a 50 percent ballast to displacement ratio, the lead is high up in the boat, and the hull form provides limited form stability. These factors conspire to necessitate reefing early on the 40. With all those hours on the wind in strong winds, I was able to experiment extensively with sail trim and reefing options. The entire trip was sailed with a flat, foam luff, 9.3 ounces, 100 percent Yankee jib (high clew—7 feet off the deck) and main. The main is the original that came with the boat. It has two rows of reef points. I have never been satisfied with the reef points in the main, feeling that neither one was deep enough. My other boats have had what I call a 1.5 and 3 reef, both of which are deeper than 'standard' reefs that most sailmakers put in. I like to put the lower reef just above the bottom batten and the second reef just above the second batten. This trip confirmed that decision for the P40."

—Chip Lawson, owner of *Passion*, P40 hull #38, describing a 450-mile passage

155

Case Study in Sailboat Shopping —Finding *Dream Keeper*

The world is not in your books and maps, it's out there.

—GANDALF

I should start by saying that, when the following episode started, I was already guilty of accumulating too many toys (read boats). The last thing I was thinking about was buying another one. Money had become tight after a career change and downsized salary, and like many others I had to start jettisoning the non-essentials to avoid a complete crash and burn. Gone was my 43-foot Formosa cutter, a rare Taiwan copy of a Ron Holland design that I was very fond of. But she had a bank loan and a big California monthly slip fee, so out she went. A few months later she was followed by my somewhat less expensive Trojan powerboat, and for the first time in twenty-five years I was not a boatowner. Nothing except two kayaks and some leftover cruising charts.

My ticket to the ocean was gone. No longer could I at least pretend that, at any moment, I was ready to untie the dock lines and plot a course for Nuku Hiva. Sweaty palms, clammy skin, moodiness, and depression set in. People talking to me were often met with a blank stare, and the only thing I could do to help with the anxiety was inventory and clean my myriad boatbuilding and maintenance tools that I had removed and kept when I sold my fleet of two boats. I realized that it is one thing to work in an office, but it is quite another to do so knowing that I no longer had my escape hatch. I realized that I was just as wedded to the idea, the concept, of owning a cruising boat as I was to the fiberglass corpus itself.

I found myself sneaking onto YachtWorld.com at my new job and longingly searching for cruising boat candidates. After all, I was just window shopping, no?

But then a house I had been trying to sell went into escrow, and I knew I had some cash coming. The job situation had improved, and I realized that it might be the perfect opportunity to put into practice the very techniques I had just submitted to my editor. A new chapter emerged, my search for the *Dream Keeper*.

I decided immediately that I would allow myself to buy another boat if I could do it using only the money that came in via my two earlier boats (after paying the bank)—about $25,000. After all, it is one thing to be addicted to sailing or the ocean, but it is quite another to let it jeopardize the financial health of your family. My oldest son was in high school, and given the choice between traveling the globe in a rolly ocean at 5 knots or continuing to explore his newest hobby—girls—well, it was not a contest. He gave me a glimmer of hope, however, that after high school we might take off for a year, and the name *Dream Keeper* was an easy pick.

It was also going to be a long escrow on the house, which was in Mexico, and I knew that it ain't sold until the money is sitting in one's bank account. So absolutely no jumping the gun. I could look but I could not touch until the bank account balance was secure.

But this was really a good thing since I knew I would have at least three months to look. And look I did, starting with California and employing the search tactics already described. Although I spent some time on craigslist, I knew that my best bet would be either YachtWorld or walking the docks at local marinas hunting down neglected boats with potential as long as the owner realized it was time to sell.

On YachtWorld I used the advanced search feature, but input only the most general of search terms. I did not specify a hull material, or even a diesel engine, but I did specify a length range of 38 to 48 feet

and a price limit of $40,000. Obviously at that price point, the list of returned search candidates would be short. After a few weeks of checking only California boats, I extended the search to Oregon and California. Even then, the search results were typically only between forty and sixty boats, with half of them wood or steel and thus ruled out immediately.

I kept an eye on a Newport 41 in San Francisco and an owner-built Corbin 39 with a decent interior. Both were well under $40,000 and had good sail inventories, but neither had radar or a quality autopilot. But my eyes kept getting drawn to the sweet lines of a cruising design I had never heard of before. It was way up in Washington State, past Bellingham and almost at the Canadian border.

The boat was called a Cartwright 40, designed in the 1970s by Allan Vaitses and built by New England Boatworks on a semi-custom basis. Although it was Vaitses who lofted the boat, he did so based on specific directions from Jerry Cartwright, a conservative former OSTAR participant who also founded the Bermuda 1-2 race and for most of his career favored full keels and heavy displacement.

While all boats are a compromise, I have always been more inclined to performance-oriented cruisers. The Cartwright 40 usually displaces over 24,000 pounds and sports a Capsize Screening Ratio of 1.61, on a par with a giant redwood. It would be a huge departure from my normal choice. But I am drawn to unique boats and have always had a fondness for flush-deck designs like the Corbin 39 or the old Pearson 40. I also knew that as I am getting older I am more inclined to favor a Cadillac ride, even if it meant that I would be in trawler mode and motorsailing more often than I would in a light air boat. If nothing else, I would pursue the Cartwright as a placekeeper boat to enjoy before finally selling the house and getting my ultimate ride into the sunset.

So as I continued to research what I could about Cartwright and his boats (he also sold a 36, a very nice 44, and eventually accepted long fin keels), I remembered one of the primary reasons I like flush-deck designs on cruising boats. It is because, in my experience, cruising successfully is all about bringing your dinghy from one anchorage to another, and the more convenient it is to launch and stow a substantial dinghy, the more fun cruising will be. So while it may be true that cruising is yacht repair in exotic ports, it is also in large part an exercise of carrying your dinghy from one place to another so you can deploy it for any manner of adventures.

Davits really are not a safe answer to carry dinghies except perhaps on a boat above 45 feet or so, and collapsing an inflatable every time you are on the move is a pain. But with a decent flush deck such as on the Cartwright, it is a snap to use a halyard to hoist even a heavy dinghy onto the foredeck—preferably onto customized chocks—and secure it easily for even a long passage. The dinghy can also then serve as a lifeboat, particularly an inflatable, since you know it is at the ready only seconds away from deployment.

Personally, I have no qualms about *coastal* cruising without a life raft if I know I have a good-quality inflatable dinghy at hand, and this can mean a savings of thousands of dollars. Since dinghy theft is a real problem in many cruising areas, on my last two cruises I have used the money I would have spent on a life raft to pay for a backup inflatable that I leave in the box stowed under a bunk or in the lazarette. If I am in a remote area, the loss of the ship's dinghy is so debilitating that I want to have a Plan B open to me. In one case I bailed out a fellow cruiser who had his dink stolen, and sold him my backup just prior to returning to San Diego.

The point here hopefully is that the easier it is to hoist, stow, or deploy the dinghy, the more fun and convenient your cruising will be. On the Cartwright 40, there were actually chocks already installed on the spacious foredeck to take a hard dinghy, and I knew it would not be difficult to get even a 9- or 10-foot dinghy stowed safely and aesthetically. This was a huge selling point for me—and one reason I was willing to overlook the cutaway full keel and probable poor performance in light air.

So I started to dig deeper. I made sure I had the original listing broker and not a co-listing or secondary broker. Then I made the first approach, via telephone anyway, to Pat McGarry of Fairhaven Yacht Sales in Bellingham, Washington.

FINAL COST TO PURCHASE AND DELIVER 1979 CARTWRIGHT 40

Initial purchase price	$22,000
Trucking from LaConner, WA, to Monterey, CA	$2,500
Agent fees for USCG documentation transfer	$300
Yard charges at LaConner Maritime to prep for trucking	$760
Pacific Northwest Rigging charges to unstep and prep mast	$850
Monterey Bay Boatworks charges to unload boat, restep mast	$800
TOTAL Landed Cost	**$27,210**

"Hi, I'm calling about the Cartwright 40 you have listed at $28,000."

"Oh yeah, great boat. What do you want to know?"

Putting aside for the moment that every boat is a "great boat" to a yacht broker, I pressed on.

"Well, I've been in sailing my whole life but never actually heard of a Cartwright 40. What can you tell me about it?"

Broker Pat went on to detail the specifics of his listing, which included a Furuno radar, a new linear polyurethane paint job, and the strong below-decks autopilot that I was looking for. The cabin sole was made of beautiful solid teak and holly strips. You could take a belt sander to it every few years and never sand through it. It was clear that this was a strong candidate for my next and possibly last sailboat.

When I finally closed escrow on my house, I phoned Gerald at Dudley Yacht Transport. The key to the entire deal would be to get the boat down the interstate at a much lower price than the typical $5,000 to $6,000.

By that time it was February. Under normal circumstances, I would have bought the boat, waited until June, and sailed her down the coast myself. But as a single parent to a teenager whose idea of purgatory was to be at sea with Dad for more than a few hours at a time, I knew that this was not in the cards. I also could not leave him on his own for the minimum two weeks needed (though he was fine with that idea), so it was either a trucking arrangement that made financial sense or else giving up.

I knew that most truckers were able to contract for a paying load in only one direction, and that they always loved to find a contract on a boat going in the direction they were already headed to avoid a "deadhead" empty trip that cost them just diesel fuel and made them no money. In other words to get paid for the round-trip if at all possible.

So I asked Gerald what he could do for me if I was not in a hurry and had a boat ready for him to go south whenever he had a contract for a boat heading north. I also told him that the beam of the boat was under 12 feet, which meant that no extra flag vehicle would be needed—something that could increase the cost at least 25 percent. Finally, I assured him that the "air draft" of the load would be under the magic 13 feet 6 inches, which is the minimum needed to drive from Seattle, Washington, to Monterey, California, without converting my prospective cruiser from a partial flush-decker into a truly flush design. I actually was not sure of the last dimension, but I figured I would cross that bridge (or more accurately go under it) if and when the purchase really went through.

When Gerald told me that he had a northbound load in San Diego waiting for him and that if I could be ready in two weeks he would halve his normal rate, things kicked into high gear. I called Pat and told him that I would buy the boat for $22,000 cash, plus I would waive the sea trial. This last step is not something I would recommend, but I knew from my research that the boat sailed acceptably and, in any event, one does not get all the feedback necessary from a one-hour sail on the protected waters of Puget Sound. So it was a calculated risk.

The next day I was e-mailed the acceptance of my offer, and I put into motion the various things that have to happen in order to truck a boat over a thousand miles without incident. Pacific Northwest

Rigging signed on for the critical procedure of unstepping the mast and loading it aboard the lowboy trailer. The furler was near-new but delicate once unrigged. To avoid kinking the aluminum sections, great care needed to be used. In addition, all the stays and turnbuckles needed to be properly labeled, electrical wires carefully cut, and so forth.

Monterey, California, would be the destination to receive my new toy, and we had to determine what the lowest clearance would be during the journey. It turned out that the only tunnel on the entire route was in the last 200 yards leading to the boatyard. But once the bowsprit was removed, we had the minimum clearance we needed, and subcontractor Jimmy Jackson (who could easily be the subject of his own reality TV show) of Florida handled it all beautifully.

So now my son and I spend the occasional weekend together working on *Dream Keeper*. The boat really just needed a thorough cleaning after years of non-use in the 100 percent humidity of Seattle. When I took her for the first sail from Monterey to Moss Landing, California, I still got the same thrill I had the first time I sailed a new-to-me boat thirty years earlier. She is certainly not perfect, with more weather helm than any other boat I have owned, and she needs a bigger prop, but she is exceedingly strong and, yes, she does pass the test as far as being an eye pleaser at anchor or under sail.

When I took her solo a few months later through the Golden Gate to her permanent berth, I knew that it might be years, and maybe never, before I could go cruising again. Even then, she was almost certainly not my final cruising boat but more of a placekeeper. But just knowing that my cruising ticket was there, in a slip three hours away from home, somehow made it all worthwhile.

Bryan Elfers prepares the purchase for a new name after arrival in Monterey, California.

References and Further Reading

Brewer, Ted. *Understanding Boat Design, Fourth Edition.* International Marine, Camden, Maine. 1993.

Calder, Nigel. *Boatowner's Mechanical and Electrical Systems, Third Edition.* International Marine, Camden, Maine. 2005.

___. *Marine Diesel Engines.* International Marine, Camden, Maine.

___. *Nigel Calder's Cruising Handook.* International Marine, Camden, Maine.

Casey, Don. *Inspecting the Aging Sailboat.* International Marine, Camden, Maine.

___. *This Old Boat, Second Edition.* International Marine, Camden, Maine. 2008.

Doane, Charles. *The Modern Cruising Sailboat.* International Marine, Camden, Maine. 2010.

Howard, Jim. *Handbook of Offshore Cruising.* Sheridan House, Dobbs Ferry, New York. 2000.

Kretschmer, John. *Sailing a Serious Ocean.* International Marine, Camden, Maine. 2013.

___. *Used Boat Notebook.* Sheridan House, Dobbs Ferry, New York. 2002.

Leonard, Beth. *The Voyager's Handbook.* International Marine, Camden, Maine. 1998.

Marchaj. *Seaworthiness, The Forgotten Factor.* International Marine, Camden, Maine.

Nestor, Gregg. *Twenty Affordable Sailboats to Take You Anywhere.* Paradise Cay Publications, Arcata, California. 2007.

Perry, Robert. *Yacht Design According to Perry: My Boats and What Shaped Them.* International Marine, Camden, Maine. 2007.

Ragle, Sharon. *The Oceans Are Waiting: Around the World on the Yacht* Tigger. Sheridan House, Dobbs Ferry, New York. 2002.

Roberts, John. *Optimize Your Cruising Sailboat.* International Marine, Camden, Maine. 2004.

Vigor, John. *The Seaworthy Offshore Sailboat.* International Marine, Camden, Maine. 2001.

Articles

Copeland, Liza and Andy. "The Beneteau First 38 after 70,000 Miles," *Blue Water Sailing*, April 2000.

Kretschmer, John. "Used Boat Notebook: The CS 36 Traditional," *Sailing* magazine, December 2002, 26–27.

The List Compared
—Some Very Subjective Conclusions

Best Performers Upwind: Newport 41, Cal 39, C & C 40

Worst Performers Upwind: Snowgoose 37, Freedom 36

Best Performers Downwind (Sheer Speed): Pearson 40, C & C 40

Worst Performer Downwind (Sheer Speed): Niagara 35

Best Performers Downwind (Seakindly Motion): Morgan 382, Snowgoose 37

Best All-Around Sailing Performance/Motion: Cal 39, C & C 40, Beneteau 38, Golden Wave 42

Worst Boat If You are Prone to Seasickness: Pearson 40

Best Boats If You are Prone to Seasickness: Snowgoose 37, Golden Wave 42

Best Build Quality: Canadian Sailcraft 36

Best Compromise between Salty Looks and Performance: Tayana 37, Morgan 382, Niagara 35, Hans Christian 38 (Telstar keel)

Best Boats for a Family Trade Winds Circumnavigation: Snowgoose 37, Beneteau 38, Golden Wave 42

Best Boats for Low Maintenance: Beneteau 38, Catalina 36, Freedom 36

Worst Boats for Low Maintenance: Hans Christian 38, Tayana 37

Best Boats for Gunkholing/Shallow Water: Snowgoose 37, Pearson 40

Best Boat to Take Over Niagara Falls: CSY 37

Best Boat for Resale Value: Tayana 37

Easiest Boats to Sail: Freedom 36, Snowgoose 37

Easiest Boats to Find: Islander 36, C & C 40

Boats That Require Closest Pre-Purchase Surveys: All, but especially the Islander, Hunter, Pearson, Snowgoose, and O'Day, as these may show structural weaknesses more readily than the rest.

Acknowledgments

The biggest advantage I enjoyed in writing this book was that nearly all the designs covered had strong owner associations, with plenty of advocates ready to contribute photos or insights about their specific model. Although in most cases this was all happening over the Internet, I could not help but think of a proud parent sitting on his living room sofa sharing pictures of his favorite child or grandchild. On occasion I had to tell a disappointed owner that the picture he had submitted was just not good enough to be used. Judging by their disappointment, you would have thought I was an admissions dean rejecting his child from a university.

Tom Wells, website coordinator for the Tartan 37, was invaluable in getting line drawings and photos to me. Jim Legere did much the same on behalf of the Hunter 37. Craig Beckwith helped on the Hans Christian 38, Rob Mazza and Rob Ball on the C&C 40, and so on. It was also great to correspond a few times with Bob Perry, whose designs are well represented here. I am sure he will not agree with all my selections, but hopefully he can appreciate that cruisers on a budget may have to settle for boats that are less than perfect but still serviceable.

Special mention has to be made to the great team at Pier 32 Marina in San Diego, a truly first-class facility led by Greg Boeh. I actually wrote a fair portion of my book there while aboard my sailboat *Strider*, and was always made to feel welcome by Greg, Bill, and Jimmy.

In Northern California, where I work as a marine surveyor, I also want to thank Teresa Camarda of Brisbane Marina, Kathy Nordendahl of Essex Credit, and Bill Hackel of New Era Yachts for their continuing support.

Finally, my brother Steve (Media Editor at *USA Today*) was invaluable in helping me with the photos and images included here. It was nice to collaborate on our first project together since, well, ever.

Index

Note: page numbers in **boldface** indicate photos or illustrations.